FOLLOW UP SALES STRATEGIES

Norm,
Wishing you a lifetime of follow up success!
Wanda

FOLLOW UP SALES STRATEGIES

How to Get More Clients and Close More Sales with a Proven Follow Up System

Editor: Adrienne Moch, adriennemoch.com
Cover design and layout by SABER Mountain Design

Printed in United States of America

ISBN 978-0-9839099-2-7

Wanda Allen • Follow Up Sales Strategies • San Diego, CA

www.followupsalesstrategies.com

FOLLOW UP SALES STRATEGIES

How to Get More Clients
and Close More Sales with a
Proven Follow Up System

Wanda Allen

This book is dedicated to my family, husband and mentors. None of this would be possible without the support each one of you has given me. I'm forever grateful.

Table of Contents

Introduction

Whether you're a salesperson, business owner or customer service representative, I have no doubt you know how important follow-up is. Most people do, but in general, so many struggle with their follow-up responsibilities. The common perception is that follow-up work is a big hairy monster, but it's not the heavy, arduous task you might think it is. I will simplify the concept of follow-up and teach you how to easily and systematically get your follow-up work done.

Throughout the book, I will reference "your business." It doesn't matter if you're self-employed or you work for someone; when I say your business, I'm talking about the business of what you do every day.

A popular quote is, "the fortune is in the follow-up." When I'm speaking, I frequently ask my audience if they've heard this quote, and every time, most people say they have. And then I'll ask who believes this quote to be true, and most say they do. I then go on to ask, *"if that's where the money is, wouldn't common sense lead you to that part of your business on a consistent basis"?* The response? I get the deer in the headlight stare. It's hard for many people to tend to the follow-up side of their business even though they know that's where the money is.

Follow-up is a much-neglected area for many professionals.

If you're one who struggles with it, I have a few theories why that is:

1. You don't think you have the time.
2. You don't know the best way to follow up with prospects and customers.
3. You don't know how often you should follow up or when you should stop.
4. You don't have a good system to support your follow-up efforts.

Some of these are mindsets that are nothing more than what you've convinced yourself to be true. This type of thinking combined with a lack of systems will stop you from taking action, which will create holes in your customer base and prospecting pipeline, leaving them vulnerable to your competition.

To self-assess your follow-up behaviors, answer the following questions:

1. Do you stay in touch with your customers and prospects as often as you should?
2. Have you ever had a prospect and/or customer ask you to call him back at a later date and you didn't?
3. Have you needed to get back to a prospect, but couldn't find the person's information or remember exactly what took place during your conversation?
4. Have you ever been embarrassed by your lack of follow-up?
5. Have you ever been in a time of need and too embarrassed to call those who can help because you haven't stayed in touch?

6. Have you ever felt you've been neglectful of your customers and prospects?
7. Does follow-up get the same priority as checking your email, voice mail and social media sites?

It's obvious what the answers *should* be to these questions. However, not being able to answer them correctly is an indicator that you need to improve your follow-up skills.

Let me ask you another set of questions:

1. Do you use a CRM/database program?
2. Do you have stacks of business cards sitting on your desk that you've done nothing with?
3. Do you have a system for inputting contacts into your CRM/database program?
4. Do you have an automated reminder system for following up and staying in touch?
5. Do you have an appreciation system in place for those who are important to you?

Again, the correct answers are obvious. If you're not able to answer them correctly, that's another indicator that you don't have good systems and processes in place for staying on top of your follow-up and staying-in-touch responsibilities. If that's the case, this book is for you.

Once you implement the *Follow Up Sales Strategies System*, you will be able to correctly answer all these questions—without a doubt.

Follow-up is a key ingredient to success and there's so much depth to it. It goes way beyond just getting back to someone when you say you will. Your customers, prospects and referral sources should **never** stop hearing from you; follow-up is something you should do forever.

While reading this book, there may be times when you squirm, cringe or maybe even get embarrassed because of your inconsistent follow-up habits. Don't worry; I'll give you plenty of ideas, tips and suggestions to implement the *Follow Up Sales Strategies System* so you can turn things around and be proud and confident in your follow-up behavior and practices.

Throughout the book, you may find yourself thinking *"I know this,"* but may I respectfully say, that I'm not interested in whether you know it; I'm interested in whether you are doing it. Just knowing something is having information and information without action does not have much value. I want you to take action. That's what this book is about, taking action by understanding, implementing and systematizing. The systems, processes and timelines I share will help you attain success at a quicker pace and easier than you ever have before.

I've spoken countless times on this subject and what I've learned from audience members is they really do want to be better in the area of follow-up. They understand its importance, but they just don't know how to do it effectively. If that's you, by the end of this book, you'll have a very clear understanding of how to be effective. There will be no more questions.

As you read through this book, you'll come to understand that follow-up is nothing more than a habit. (You'll see that I use the word habit often throughout the book.) Good or bad, habits always produce results. High-level performers have good habits. If you're struggling with your performance, you just need to improve your habits. Excellence is nothing more than a habit. Habits are very powerful. When something is a habit, you have control over it.

The following poem illustrates the power of habits:

You may know me…I'm your constant companion
I'm your greatest helper
I'm your heaviest burden
I will push you onward…or drag you down to failure

I am at your command if you choose to use me
Half the tasks you do…can be turned over to me
I'm able to do them quickly and I'm able to do them the same every time

I'm easily managed...all you have to do is be firm with me
Show me exactly how you want it done
After a few lessons, I'll do it automatically

I am the servant of all great men and women and of course the servant of all the failures as well
I've made all the great individuals who have ever been great and all the losers too.

I work with the precision of a computer and the intelligence of a human being
You may run me for profit or you may run me to ruin
It makes no difference to me
Take me. Be easy with me and I will destroy you
Be firm with me and I'll put the world at your feet.
Who am I?

I AM YOUR HABIT

— Author Unknown

Yes, habits are powerful and they can have a significant impact on your life. It's important for you to be open to establishing new habits that will replace ones that aren't serving you well and in fact may be preventing you from attaining all the success that is possible.

I want you to take ownership of where you are in your business right now. Be honest. If you're not where you want to be, what are you doing or not doing that is contributing to your situation? Before you start finger pointing, blaming the economy, your company, the industry, your boss, your team, or any other person or thing, I'm going to ask you to first look within. What I teach in this book will support you in taking control over your production/performance. You can make great strides in your business and life simply by changing your habits. Stay away from blaming external circumstances. I want you to take the power back.

I created the *Follow Up Sales Strategies System* and have been using it for years. I've experienced amazing results and have accomplished many great goals as a result of the system. I share my successes not to try to impress you, but to show you how the system will support you in achieving success.

This system is tried, tested and true. I want you to implement it and let it work its magic in your business. It will truly liberate you from the daily difficulties that come from poor follow-up habits. You'll rid yourself of feeling scattered, embarrassed, frustrated and guilty—negative emotions that are a heavy load to carry around every day, weighing you down and stealing your joy.

I want you to get your energy back and start enjoying every day. When you learn how to consistently get your follow-up work done, it changes everything. Your negative emotions will be replaced with positive ones such as appreciation, confidence, organization and discipline. You'll turn into a person who is skilled at follow-up, which will result in business growth and creating and retaining relationships that are important to you. You'll see why and how this happens in the pages to come.

In Part I of this book, I'm going to lay a foundation of understanding about the importance of follow-up and what it really means. I want to deepen your knowledge about it. Most people have just a shallow understanding about it, and I don't want you to be a shallow thinker on this topic. My goal in Part I is for you to gain a completely different perspective on follow-up and understand it so well that you are totally committed to implementing the *Follow Up Sales Strategies System*, which is detailed in Part II.

In Part II, my intent is to simplify the follow-up process for you and give you a roadmap to implement to suit your specific needs. When you understand follow-up's true meaning, the whole process will be easier, and exciting as well. You'll go from dreading your follow-up work to looking forward to that part of your day.

In Part II, you'll learn how to:

- Implement systems
- Use timelines
- Use effective scripting

If you're open to learning new practices, developing new habits, and committed to making changes, then let's get started.

Part I

Chapter 1
You're Sitting on a Goldmine

I know without a doubt that you are sitting on a goldmine of potential success with the people you know, the relationships you have and the connections you've made. The opportunities are there for you. But, to be able to tap into your goldmine, you've got to have good follow-up habits and systems in place. When you learn how to do that, you will be able to easily and comfortably tap into your goldmine.

The beauty of this is you don't have to always be looking for *new* prospects and customers. While meeting new people is always good, it's not your be all and end all for building your prospect and customer base. You probably don't realize all the potential you're sitting on with people you already know. I want you to be able to go get the opportunities that are there waiting for you—and follow-up is the way to do it.

Go Get Your Lost Relationships

You may be thinking *"my goldmine isn't as big as it should be because I've let a lot of relationships go."* No worries; you can bring lost relationships back into your goldmine. Many people feel that rekindling relationships is too uncomfortable, so they don't do it. It's not uncomfortable at all if you're using the right verbiage. It doesn't matter how long its been since you've talked to the person; your opening dialog will always be the same. It's a three-step process:

1. Admit you haven't stayed in touch.
2. Apologize for it.
3. Move on to the purpose of your call.

When you make the rekindling call, the purpose is for no other reason than to reconnect. You're not going to ask for business, referrals or anything else. You don't want the person you're calling to think the only reason you're contacting him is to get something. That's not very impressive.

Scripting

Hi Joe, this is Karen. I know it's been forever since we've talked and I'm sorry I haven't stayed in touch. I was thinking about you and wanted to call and see how you're doing.

The conversation will take its course from there.

There's no need for you to be uncomfortable because Joe didn't stay in touch with you, either. If you had a connection with him, more than likely, he'll be happy to hear from you. Then you can put him in your staying in touch system (discussed in Part II), so you won't forget about him again.

Follow-up Is Critically Important to Success

Follow-up is a fundamental in the sales process, but too often, it's a neglected fundamental. It's one that's easy not to do. You can network, prospect, get appointments, make presentations and negotiate, but if you're not following up, all those efforts are for naught.

What are your follow-up efforts once business has been

transacted? Following up after the sale has closed is vitally important to continued success. Oftentimes, there's more business to be had with customers and even if there's not, they most likely know people who can use your services. Closing a sale is not a reason to stop following up.

According to thesaurus.com, words that are synonymous with follow-up are:

- Check out
- Find out
- Look into
- Investigate
- Make sure
- Pursue

According to thesaurus.com, words that are antonyms to follow-up are:

- Avoid
- Dodge
- Forget

I find both the synonyms and antonyms very telling. These should shed some light on your perspective of what following up or not following really does. When you don't tend to your follow-up work, you are literally avoiding, dodging and forgetting about your prospects and customers. How can you build your business or improve your production when you're acting this way?

On the flip side, when you are following up, you're looking into, making sure, pursuing and checking out. These are words that reflect due diligence, taking your prospects and customers seriously and making the necessary efforts to build your business, increase your production, and strengthen your relationships.

Opportunity Knocks

One of *my* synonyms to follow-up is opportunity. When you have follow-up work to do that means you have opportunities waiting for you. Opportunity is a matter of perception. You may view something as an opportunity, while someone else may consider the same thing to be an obstacle or difficult task. If you look at follow-up as opportunity, it will change your attitude and energy toward it. I talk to a lot of people about their follow-up work and I can literally see them shrink before my eyes with their body language. When I see this, I know they view follow-up as an obstacle that's heavy and difficult. If this is you, I encourage you to shift your viewpoint to opportunity. It will have a positive impact on your productivity.

Surprising Sales Statistics

48% of salespeople never follow-up.
80% of sales are made between the 5th & 12th contact.
Only 10% of salespeople make more than 3 contacts.

Source:
National Sales Executive Assoc.

These sales statistics show just how much salespeople struggle with follow-up. By the end of this book, you'll learn how to be in the elite 10%.

Let's discuss each of these statistics in further detail.

48% of Salespeople Never Follow-up

Based on the work I've done and the countless conversations

I've had with people about their follow-up habits, I believe this statistic is worse than 48%. Why? One very common problem most people have is collecting business cards and doing nothing with them. This is an indicator that no follow-up action has been taken. It is a rare occasion when I'm told someone doesn't have business cards stacked up. I'd say 95% of those I talk to have this problem, which means they're not following up. Couple that with not staying in touch with existing prospects and customers and it can easily be determined that more than 48% never follow-up.

If you have business card buildup, don't worry. We'll discuss this in Follow-up Must #1 and then I'll teach you how to prevent it from happening in System #2.

At an event, I sat next to a woman who was a social media expert with a primary client base of speakers and authors. I was interested in her services and she said she would follow up with me to set a time to talk further. At the end of the event, she told me again that she would follow up. I never heard from her. I wonder how often she does that and how much business she loses because she doesn't follow up.

80% of Sales are Made Between the 5th & 12th Contact

I track my contacts very closely and I am spot on with 80% of my sales being made between the 5th and 12th contact. I wish I could say it was different, but it's not. If you've made multiple contacts with a prospect and you still don't have his or her business, remind yourself of these statistics. There's no need to get discouraged. It's not you; it's what research tells us.

It's normal to be disappointed after an unsuccessful contact, but you must promptly shake that feeling. If you carry it around for too long, it will turn into discouragement, which is a heavy load. It can be a showstopper. It's hard to move forward when you're discouraged, so let the disappointment roll off you like water off a duck's back.

Only 10% of Salespeople Make More Than 3 Contacts

Another way of looking at this statistic is that 90% of salespeople make two contacts with a prospect and then quit. If you're only making two contacts and 80% of sales are made between the 5th and 12th contact, you're walking away from business and leaving it for someone else to get when the prospect is ready.

There are two primary reasons why 90% quit after two tries:

1. They assume the prospect isn't interested. If you make this assumption, you are in essence making the buying decision for the prospect.

2. They don't have systems in place. To follow up with someone for the 5th, 9th or 12th time, you must have systems in place that will support that many contacts. I'll teach you how to do that. With the *Follow Up Sales Strategies System*, you can follow up until the end of time and never lose track of anyone.

I decided in October that I would have myself videotaped during one of my speaking engagements that was to be held in January. I was in need of a video for my website. I spoke to two video professionals in October and told them I would be ready for their services in January.

The first person I spoke to was very friendly and informative about his services. When I told him what my timing was, I could hear the excitement leave his voice. He said he would email me some information, which he never did. He also told me he would contact me in January, and he didn't do that, either.

The second person I spoke to was very friendly and gave me some good information about her services. I told her what my timing was and she said she would contact me in January. Guess what? I never heard from her.

Because of the lack of follow up with these two professionals, I was forced to look elsewhere, in other words, to their competitors. I spoke to a third person. I was pleased with the description of his services and pricing. He said he would send me a proposal the next day. I didn't get it until the following week; he never called to tell me there would be a delay and didn't even acknowledge it when he sent it to me. Because he was late, I was forced, yet again, to look for another video person. His inability to keep his word on getting me the proposal left me with a poor impression of how he does business. I wasn't willing to take that risk. I love the saying "how you do anything is how you do everything." It keeps situations like this in perspective for me.

I had to look for yet another video person. I put out feelers and was referred to a woman named Corrie. She responded promptly to my inquiry and I had a quote within 24 hours. I knew with this kind of service, she was the one I would hire.

I had to go through three people to find one who would follow up properly and provide good service. The fact that the first two didn't call me back told me they don't have an effective follow-up system in place. Had one of them responded and provided good service, I would have been guaranteed business. Unfortunately, they both missed out and let their competitor get my business.

Here's another story that will show you how critical it is to not give up after two contacts.

I was speaking at an event and a gentleman named Tim came up to me afterward to get my contact information. He told me he works for an insurance company and thought his manager might be interested in one of my workshops. He said he would talk to her about it. I asked him if it would be OK if I followed up with him, and then got his contact information.

I asked for his permission to follow up in case I didn't hear from him. I'll talk further about how critical it is to have follow-up conversations in Chapter 7.

I followed up with him several times. It took six contacts and three months to get his manager's contact information.

You would think it would have taken no time at all to get his manager's information, but as you now know, 80% of the time, it takes five or more contacts. It would have been easy to assume that either Tim decided not to refer me to his manager or he did refer me and his manager wasn't interested. But, I'm not in the 90% who assumes or quits after two contacts, so I kept on keeping on.

Once I got the manager's contact information, I began to follow up with her. It took four contacts and five months to get the green light to submit a proposal for my workshop. I could hear in her voice that she was excited about booking me. I submitted the proposal. It took another month and three contacts to find out it had been approved. In that third contact, she told me she would email some potential dates for the workshop. I was thinking, *"this is a done deal,"* but it wasn't. I followed up five more times over a six-month period before I talked to her again. After the first month, not every contact was about booking the workshop. It was time to start mixing up my contacts because she had gone "cold" on me. I didn't want every contact at this point to be about the workshop. We were in the middle of a holiday season, so I sent her a holiday card, emailed some sales information and continued to follow up about the workshop. (I'll talk about mixing up your contacts in Part II.) I had no idea what happened or why she went cold, because the last time we spoke, she was ready to book a date. At this point, my goal was to make sure I reminded her that I was still around; I didn't want her to forget about me.

It could have been very easy to assume she was no longer interested. However, I knew the last time we had spoken, she was interested and ready to book a date. I had not heard anything to the contrary. I couldn't make any assumptions and therefore the only option I had was to continue with my follow-up efforts. This is how you keep yourself in the game.

One day I'm in my office and the phone rings. Lo and behold, it's the manager. She apologizes for the delay and tells me what caused it. It had absolutely nothing to do with her level of interest. There were circumstances beyond anyone's control that created the delay. (This is why you can never assume.) We booked a date and I taught the workshop to her sales team of 80. This is a high profile company in San Diego and to have the following testimonial from one of the principals is a very big deal and a powerful prospecting tool. (I'll discuss the power of testimonials in Part II) This never would have happened had I made assumptions or quit after two contacts.

"One of the hardest tasks our salespeople have to do is get that first meeting. Wanda's ***Follow Up Sales Strategies*** *training provided our team a proven system for making that initial contact. Many of our business development professionals have changed how they approach prospecting. They are now scheduling the time and are more persistent in their follow-up."*

— Trindl Reeves, Principal, Barney & Barney

In total, it took 15 months and 13 contacts between Tim and Trindl to get this business. My mindset is that I have the time for this process because I know I'm going to be in business a long time. I don't get caught up in the number of contacts I have to make and I have systems in place to support my follow-up efforts.

I want you to make a decision right now that you will no longer quit after two contacts or make assumptions when you're prospecting.

Follow-up Systems That Don't Work

If you aren't consistent with your follow-up efforts, one primary reason is because you're not using the right system. There's a strong likelihood you're using one or more of the following systems that do not work.

Spiral Notebook on Your Desk

You'll spend too much time sifting through pages looking for notes you wrote who knows when. What if you lost the notebook? There goes your follow-up system. How much money would be lost in potential business?

Sticky Notes

Not good at all. Sticky notes tend to get scattered, lost or misplaced. You could have a $1,000,000 sticky that gets lost. What a shame that would be.

Email

It doesn't matter how organized you are with your email folders, it's still not a good system. It takes too much time when you have to go through multiple emails or a chain of emails.

Word or Excel

While these are better than a spiral notebook or sticky notes, neither is a good system. These programs aren't automated, which leaves too much room for error and oversight.

Your Head

This is the worst of the worse systems, but unfortunately is one that's very commonly used. You can't store your follow-up information in your head. Life is busy and I'm sure you'll agree, there's not much room available in your brain to effectively store valuable follow-up information. This is the system that wakes you up at 3 a.m. thinking, *"I can't believe I forgot to do that."*

If you're using any of these systems or a number of them, you're only going to get so far before it becomes unmanageable and you become overwhelmed—and that likely means you won't continue to use it. Another problem with these systems is they're big time wasters. There's no order or organization to any of them. If you're using one or more of these systems, I'm going to ask you to be willing to let them go. Be committed to implementing a system that will be efficient, timesaving and productive. I'll discuss how you do that in Part II.

How Well Do You Invest?

Do you do a good job investing in your relationships? If not, you can correct this by improving your follow-up efforts. Follow-up is nothing more than your willingness to invest in your relationships. It doesn't matter if your relationship is with a prospect, customer, referral source or vendor. If someone is important to you, you should be investing in that person on a consistent basis.

Think about things from a prospecting standpoint. Let's say you meet someone who's interested in your product/service, but it's not a good time for this person to buy. He asks you to follow up next month. You should look at this as a new opportunity and a new relationship in which you're willing to invest. It's exciting, because follow-up is more than an investment; it's a chance to create a good impression. Those with whom you consistently invest will be left with a positive impression of you—and when you invest well, the dividends are great payoffs.

Follow-up is the Lost Art of Customer Service

I'm sure you'll agree with me that the customer service bar is very low today. To be frank, it's terrible. You can be hard-pressed to consistently find good customer service these days. And by the way, customer service applies to everyone you interact with, including prospects, referral sources, vendors, receptionists and fellow staff members. When you implement the *Follow Up Sales Strategies System*, your customer service skills will become exceptional. You will stand out and be head and shoulders above the masses.

Go Beyond the Prospecting Phase

I mentioned earlier that there is a shallow understanding of follow-up. Most people relate follow-up to the prospecting phase and believe once business has been transacted, they no longer need to follow up and stay in touch with their customers. Does this sound like you? Once business has been transacted, are you off looking for your next new lead, prospect or customer—forgetting about those with whom you've already done business? When you drop your relationships after a deal is done, you're walking away from potentially more business and/or the opportunity for referrals. This is tragic, especially if you're not interacting with satisfied customers. Don't walk away from people with whom you have an approval rating. This is really important. To do nothing with them is a disservice to both you and your customers.

Staying in Touch After the Sale

There is an extension of following up that's called staying in touch. I discovered this concept when I was a banker.

I had a 25-year banking career and specialized in the area of SBA lending, which is where I spent the lion's share of those years. Five years before I left banking, I was asked if I would consider the position of Branch Manager. I had been managing SBA departments for 15 years and was ready for a change, so I took on the challenge. The reason I viewed it as a challenge is because it was going to put me on the sales side of banking. Not only was I going to have my own sales goals, but I also was going to be responsible for the branch's sales goals. Shortly after taking the position, I got my first big prospect. It was a company that had seven-figure deposits and good lending needs. In the banking business, this is golden. We were in competition with two other banks and part of the business owner's decision process was having his office manager (Jill) interview the three of us bankers. In that interview, she asked me, *"are you going to be one of those bankers who we always hear from in the beginning and then you get our business and we never hear from you again?"*

Let me ask you a question:

- Have you ever done business with someone and once the transaction was over, you never heard from the person again?

Now I want to turn that question around:

- Have you ever done business with a customer and once the transaction was over, you never contacted that person again?

It doesn't matter what side of the fence you're on in this scenario; it's not a good feeling.

When Jill asked me that question, I told her, "*no, I'm not one of those bankers who don't stay in touch after business has been closed.*" Truth be told, I had no idea what kind of banker I was. I knew what kind of SBA Manager I was, but hadn't defined myself in my new role. However, I'm not dumb. I knew what the right answer was and what she wanted to hear, which is what I told her. I made a note to myself, "if you get the business, figure out how to consistently stay in touch after the deal has been closed." We did get the business, so I needed to figure that out. As mentioned before, I spent the majority of my banking career managing SBA departments, and if you know anything about SBA loans, you know they're loaded with rules and regulations because they're government loans. I figured out early in my career that if I was going to run a smooth operation and pass annual audits, I had to have good systems in place. Because of this, I developed a knack for creating systems and became very good at it. Thus, in the midst of my quandary about how I could consistently stay in touch with my new customer, I fell back on what I knew how to do, which was create systems. I developed systems for following up on the prospecting side and staying in touch once the business was closed, hence the birth of *Follow Up Sales Strategies.*

As mentioned earlier, I've used these systems for years. They're tried, tested and true. Trust me throughout the process of this book and you'll see how well they work!

Secure Powerful Relationships

In the course of my career, which includes working with many successful clients, I've developed the opinion that the most successful people have the best relationships. I'm sure you'll agree with me that it's impossible to have a good relationship with someone if you're not staying in touch. That's common sense, but not all too common. People are losing touch with their relationships more and more today and the reason given for that is often the same: *"I'm so busy, I don't have time to stay in touch."* This is unfortunate. At the end of the day, you do business with people. If you're not staying in touch with the people who are important to you, you will not have secure, powerful relationships.

I want to caution you not to fall into the trap of thinking that because you stay in touch through social media, text or email, your relationships are good. NOT. If you are only staying in touch through electronic means, there's not going to be a lot of depth to your relationships. They will go only so far. It doesn't matter how great and amazing technology gets; it will never replace verbal communication, a smile, a handshake or a hug. We are human beings and human interaction is crucial to the well-being of our relationships.

Following up is a great way to secure *new* powerful relationships. I want you to think beyond securing the relationships you already have, which is vitally important, but understand that you can also secure powerful relationships with people you don't know or haven't met. The following story will help you understand how this works.

> I was out for a jog one day and as I'm running, I noticed a number of business cards laying on the road. I could tell they were the same person's business cards because I could see the logo was the same on all of them. I had an inkling to pick one up, but I ignored it. As I ran further up the road, I saw more of the same business cards. This time I didn't ignore my inkling and I picked up one. The person was a National Recruiting Director for a finance company named Jim. Of course, my first thought was I needed to meet him. I sent him a card and explained how I came across his business card. I briefly described my business and told him I would follow up to see if he'd be interested in my services. After a couple of days, I called him. He took my call, but was very short with the conversation. He said he might be interested, but told me I would be on the backburner. I told him I understood and asked if I could follow up. He said yes and I continued to follow up with him over the next three months. I made eight contacts and each time we talked he got friendlier and friendlier and the initial "shortness" I felt in our first conversation slowly disappeared. We continued to have conversations about my services, but he wasn't ready.

Chapter 2
Developing Follow-up Habits

As I've already said, following up is nothing more than a habit and there are numerous facets to it. Some of what I'm about to share may seem elementary, but as simple as it may seem, I must discuss each area, because what is perceived as being basic and common is not so common. If you can get back to the fundamentals of common courtesy, taking care of your relationships, and keeping your word, you'll be head and shoulders above your competition by practicing the basics.

What Kind of an Impression Do You Leave?

Everything you do leaves an impression...good or bad. Understanding this concept should help you be mindful of your tone of voice, attitude, friendliness, commitments and everything else you do when working with others. You should *want* to be impressionable. This will give you a competitive edge when it comes time for a prospect's buying decision. If you've impressed the prospect and your competition hasn't, guess who gets the business: you. As I mentioned earlier, the customer service bar is so low, it doesn't take much to leave a good impression or "wow" those you're working with. That's great news for you. Treat everyone like a $1,000,000 customer and imagine the kind of impression you would leave.

Actions Speak Louder Than Words

Are you a person of your word? Do you do what you say you're going to do when you say you're going to do it? If you can just get this one habit down, it can have a great impact on your business. So often in this crazy busy world we live in, people are accustomed to not doing what they say they will. And worse, that is becoming acceptable. Be a person of your word and keep your commitments.

Are You Late?

Being late doesn't leave a good impression *ever*, especially if it's habitual. Being late can become a habit. You can get so accustomed to it that it's not a big deal and doesn't bother you. However, being late is disrespect toward others. It's showing you're not concerned with their time. When you're late, you're not doing what you said you would do. When you agree to meet someone at a certain time, it's important to keep your word. Do you want to be seen as the person who is always a few minutes early or the person who runs in late gasping for air, apologizing and explaining your tardiness? Which impression do you want to make?

Make a commitment to yourself that from this day forward you will do whatever it takes to always be five minutes early for every appointment.

How Long Does it Take to Return Calls, Emails, Texts?

There are some time management philosophies that advocate returning phone calls/texts and checking emails during certain times of the day. I'm going to give you another perspective on this. I certainly understand you can't drop whatever you're doing every time your phone rings or an email or text comes in. However, you can manage communication effectively by responding to the email, text or phone call at your earliest convenience, remaining responsive to the person contacting you. Take on the mindset that business is more about your customers/prospects/referral sources than it is about you. I'm not saying to let them manage you, but you do need to create a time management system that takes exceptional customer service into consideration.

Don't you love working with people who get back to you in a timely fashion, those who always respond promptly to your question, call or concern? It establishes a great sense of trust and confidence in knowing your need will be taken care of. Don't you want your "people" to feel that good about you? Your prospects, customers and referral sources are the lifeline to your business. Take care of them with prompt responses.

Are You *Always* Friendly?

This doesn't mean you're happy and friendly 24/7. What it means is you're always friendly when communicating with your customers, prospects and referral sources. Regardless of what's going on with you, these people deserve to be treated in a friendly manner. When you're always friendly, those you're working with won't have to deal with inconsistent moods or feel as if they're bothering you. I'm sure you've had a customer service experience when the person you're dealing with was unfriendly. It's not pleasant. Don't be that person or give that experience to your customers. Be stable…be friendly.

The saying, "kill 'em with kindness" is powerful. It's very hard to be mad, frustrated or upset with someone who's kind and friendly. If you have a reputation for always being friendly, you'll be granted much more forgiveness in any given situation than someone who's not. If you or your company makes an error, it will be much easier for your customers to forgive the situation because of the friendly way you've always handled the relationship. Most times, kindness will trump problems and difficulty.

If you're a business owner and have a receptionist, it's very important to make sure that person represents you well and is friendly from the word hello. You can absolutely hear a smile over the phone. Receptionists are the first impression of a business.

Put a smiley face on your desk to remind yourself to *always* be friendly.

Chapter 3
Mindset Shifts to Support New Skills

So many of our problems we create in our own mind. I want you to get out of your head. Focus on your actions, your systems and your goals. This will keep your mind from running away on you and creating unfounded thoughts that prevent you from taking action and being your best.

Stick to the facts of any situation you're facing and don't let your mind create fictitious information that prevents you from moving forward with what needs to be done. Your mind is very powerful and you have to be aware of the thoughts that are swirling around in it. Ask yourself if your thoughts are accurate, supportive and contributing to your success. If the answer is no, dump the thought. You have to be conscious and aware of your thoughts if you're going to effectively challenge them and get rid of those that don't serve and support you and your success.

Don't Be Weighed Down by Your Follow-up Work

As mentioned earlier, so many view follow-up work as heavy and cumbersome. It literally weighs them down, creating what I call "the boulder on the shoulder." When you're going through each day with a boulder on your shoulder, it's exhausting; it will weigh you down and zap your energy. The system I'm going to teach you will lighten your load and put a spring in your step.

I was speaking at an event and I asked the audience to shout out words that are synonymous with follow-up. The first few words were relationships, prospects and commitments, which are all good words. Then a gentleman in the back of the room yelled out *"pain in the butt,"* and the audience cheered. He was honest and the rest of the crowd clearly supported his sentiment. If you would have cheered after his comment, I want to remind you that follow-up is opportunity. That's it. Nothing more, nothing less. As I've already said, if you don't view follow-up as opportunity, you'll view it as a heavy task that will weigh you down. Release the "boulder on your shoulder" by shifting your mindset to note that follow-up is opportunity.

Don't Get Emotional

Emotions can really cause problems. More times than not, the follow-up emotions you experience are the direct result of your thoughts that have little to do with reality. If you get too emotional about your follow-up efforts, you run the risk of not taking necessary action.

What do follow-up emotional thoughts look like?

I don't know if I should follow up.

I'm not sure if the prospect is interested.

I feel like I'm bothering the prospect.

I don't want to be a pest.

I don't want the prospect to think I'm a stalker.

Stalker may seem like a strong word, but I've heard this comment from many people. Unfortunately, this is how they view themselves during the prospecting process.

As you now know, 90% of salespeople quit after two contacts. I've said the two primary reasons are because they make assumptions and they don't have good systems. Another reason is emotions kick in as a result of the thoughts noted above. If you're having these thoughts, they're going to turn into emotion and could very well stop you from taking action. One of the many beauties of having a follow-up system in place is it pulls the emotion out of the process. It's not about what you think or feel; it's about your system. Your system is your guiding force rather than your emotions.

In Part II, I'll teach you a tactic for keeping your thoughts/ emotions at bay simply by having follow-up conversations.

Have you ever heard that when emotions go up, intelligence goes down? I believe this is 100% true with follow-up. The more emotional you get, the greater chance there is of you not taking action, which reflects a decline in intelligence.

When you hear yourself having any of the emotional thoughts noted, tell yourself "STOP."

Slow Down

We live in such a fast-paced world today that people are busier than they've ever been, and that leads to operating from an immediate mindset. An immediate mindset is one that thinks, *"I don't have time or I'm too busy."* This is very dangerous thinking. Just because you're busy can't be a reason not to do your follow-up work. Ideally you *want* to be busy because that means you have a thriving business.

When you read the sales statistics mentioned earlier that

80% of sales are made between the 5th & 12th contact, you might have thought *"there's no way I have time to follow up with someone that many times."* Let me ask you a question that will challenge that thought. *"Do you plan on being in the same business or industry, or with the same company three months, six months, a year or however long it will take to convert the prospect to a customer"?* If the answer is yes, I'm going to say you do have the time. You just have to make the time, and I'll discuss how you do that in Chapter 7. Thinking you're too busy and don't have time to follow-up is keeping you in the immediate mindset and will prevent you from getting future business. Discard those thoughts.

Another thing that feeds the immediate mindset is a thin pipeline. When your pipeline is thin, you may think, *"I don't have time for multiple follow-ups because I've got to go find that prospect who's ready to go now."* How often does that happen? Not very. Building your business is a marathon, not a sprint. Have you ever heard, "the one who's in a hurry loses"? That's 100% true with follow-up. If you believe you're too busy to follow-up, you'll lose the business and leave it for someone else.

Chapter 4
Prioritizing Is Critical to Your Follow-up Success

The #1 reason why people tell me they can't get their follow-up work done is because they don't have the time. I've heard it a million times, but I don't ever believe it. I don't care who the person is, what his or her life situation is or what industry he or she is in, it's never about the time. The reason follow-up work doesn't get done is because it doesn't have a high enough priority. When your follow-up work isn't a priority, you'll do it when you can; when you think about it; when you have the time; and worst of all, when you're in the mood. Who's ever in the mood to do follow-up work? Probably no one. It should be something you just do because it's part of every workday.

I can pretty much guarantee you that regardless of how busy you are, you would never go a day without checking your email, voicemail or text messages. If you did, you'd probably have a hard time sleeping. That's where I want follow-up to be for you. In other words, if you went a day without doing your follow-up work, it would keep you up at night. You don't wait to check your email, voicemail or text messages until you have the time, are in the mood or think about it. You just do it because it's part of your day.

Are You Really Too Busy?

You shouldn't be surprised when I tell you you're not too busy. You get done what's on your list of priorities. Stephen Covey has four time management quadrants. One of them is important, but not urgent. I believe that's where most people file follow-up. I don't ever have to tell anyone how important follow-up is. That's common knowledge, but there's no urgency attached to it. I'm not saying it needs to be a red hot, on fire urgent matter. But there does have to be some degree of urgency attached to it so it will move up your priority list. Getting it prioritized will eliminate the "I'm too busy" excuse. In Part II, you'll learn how to prioritize.

Stop Looking For More Time

Do you feel like you're always looking for more time? Let me relieve you of this bad habit. There's no more time for you to find. You get just 24 hours a day, and that's all you'll ever get. We're all given the same amount of time. How you choose to use it is entirely up to you. We all have different life circumstances, but if you're in a business-building or sales production career, making time for follow-up is imperative. When you convince yourself you don't have time, you're pushing away your customers, prospects and referral sources. You have to be strategic in how you spend your time. Structure your day and make sure follow up is on your list of priorities.

The busier your life is, the more critical it is to implement the *Follow Up Sales Strategies System*. It will help keep your business life streamlined, more efficient and productive.

Two Reasons to Follow-up

1. Build Your Business

2. Strengthen Your Relationships

If you're not spending focused, quality time every working day following up, you're not spending focused, quality time building your business and building your relationships. If you go a day, a week or a few weeks without following up, think about the business and relationships you're jeopardizing. Follow-up is something you should do every workday—forever. You should never stop following up and staying in touch with those who are important to you.

When you tell yourself you don't have time to follow-up, what you're really saying is, *"I don't have time to build my business or strengthen my relationships."* I'm sure you'll agree with me, this thought makes no sense. The reason you get up and go to work is to build your business. You may not have realized that strengthening your relationships should be a part of your day as well. You'll fully understand this concept as you keep reading.

Are You Afraid of the Two-Letter Word?

I strongly believe many people use the *"I don't have time"* mindset as an excuse to not do their follow-up work because what they're really afraid of is hearing that two-letter word: no. An excuse is nothing more than a "cover story" or a "cop out." It's not the real truth. Let's be honest; when you follow up, you open yourself up to rejection and that's scary for a lot of people. The fact of the matter is the more you follow up, the more you'll be told no. There's no escaping it. But what I want you to understand is being told no is part of the process to be successful. Bottom line, you can't be afraid to be told no. No is progress; it's an update. For this reason, I'll take a no over being ignored any day of the week. One thing I can guarantee is if you don't follow up, you surely won't get the business. You'll protect yourself from hearing the word no and you'll also protect yourself from hearing the word yes.

I've done research on closing ratios. What I surmise is 35-50% is considered a good closing range, and it varies based on industry, sales cycle, and other factors. Given this range, to be good at closing, you're going to miss 50-65% of the time.

Baseball legend Ted Williams is quoted as saying, *"those who fail '**only**' seven times out of 10 attempts will be the greatest in the game,"* and it turns out he was right when you look at the batting averages of the best hitters. Notice, he said *only* seven times. In other words, if you get a hit three times out of 10, you're going to be extraordinary. Thus, to be successful, you have to miss or in other words, be told no. It's part of the process. Imagine getting three customers out of every 10 prospects. How would that impact your business?

Remind yourself that when you're following up, the absolute worst thing that can happen is either the prospect will be rude or you'll be told no—and neither of these responses is life shattering. You'll survive, the sun will rise and you will carry on. I promise. The more you do this, the thicker your skin will get.

If a prospect is rude, tell yourself it's not about you and don't take it personally. There's something going on in that person's life that's creating a down mood. Another approach when someone is rude is to mentally thank the prospect for behaving in a way that lets you determine this is not a person you want to pursue and do business with. Remove this individual from your pipeline and move on.

The second worst thing that can happen is you'll be told no. You now know this is part of the journey to being successful and you shouldn't be afraid of it. If you're not willing to be told no, you're not willing to be successful.

I'm not saying you shouldn't *ever* be nervous, uncomfortable or hesitant before you follow up. But you can't let those feelings stop you from taking action. The only thing you have control over is your actions. Do what you need to do and the rest will take care of itself.

Chapter 5
Powerful Results of Effective Follow-up

If you embrace the teachings of this book, you're going to experience the powerful results that I'm going to share with you. Every one of these will have a significant impact on your business.

Result #1

Gain Strong Relationships

If you really look at success, doesn't it boil down to relationships? Yes, you have to be good at what you do and knowledgeable about your products or services, but that's not going to guarantee a strong relationship. The only way to guarantee a strong relationship is to consistently invest in it. The more investments you make, the stronger the relationship will be. When you've invested well, your relationships can be a great resource for you.

I have a client named Andre who has owned his insurance agency for 25 years. That's a long time to be in business, which means he had accumulated a lot of customers over the years. When I started working with Andre, my first thought was *"your goldmine is huge."* But, because insurance is a recurring business, as with many in a recurring business, there's a tendency to forget about the goldmine. When policies renew consistently, it's easy to go on autopilot. I told Andre he could tap into the customer base he already has by implementing some systems that will support his staying in touch efforts and enhance his opportunities to get more business from current customers. Many of these people have done business with him for years and were ripe for Andre to sell new products or ask for referrals. We implemented some staying in touch systems and it wasn't long before he started seeing an increase in business.

"It was a pleasure working with Wanda! She has been instrumental in helping me see what I need to do to maximize the opportunities with my insurance agency. During our coaching sessions, we developed strategies and systems to consistently maintain contact with prospects, new customers and long-time customers. Utilizing these systematic approaches has made a positive impact on my bottom line and has increased my customer base. I only wish I had met her years ago."

— Andre Padilla, State Farm Agent

When you develop the habit of consistently following up and staying in touch, you're going to have strong relationships. As I said earlier, you can't have a good relationship if you're not staying in touch. Your relationships are like a plant; they must be watered and cared for. If they're left untended, they'll wither away and die.

You can gauge how strong your relationship is with anyone by asking yourself the following question:

Am I comfortable picking the phone up and calling for any reason?

If the answer is no and you deem that person as important, it's time to start investing more. In Part II, I'll teach you many different ways to invest in your relationships. Once you've implemented the *Follow Up Sales Strategies System*, you will consistently stay in touch with ease and order.

If I'm in the prospecting phase and a prospect tells me no, I don't necessarily let that relationship go—especially if I've invested enough time to the point that I have a relationship with the prospect. Do you get told no and drop the relationship? If so, this is a mistake and not good business, because situations change. What used to be too much, too inconvenient or not the right time can change next month, next quarter or next year. If the situation does change, you want to be the person that prospect thinks about, and the only way for that to happen is to stay in touch. I suggest you get the prospects' permission to stay in periodic touch after they've told you no. (See the following scripting.)

I'm not suggesting you stay in touch with every prospect who tells you no. You should limit your staying in touch efforts to the ones with whom you've established a relationship. To make it really simple, just ask yourself, *"do I like this person?"* If the answer is yes, don't let the prospect go. Even if your relationship never culminates in business, if you invest wisely, this person may be a referral source.

Let's say you're in the insurance business and you have a prospect you've been following up with for months. She made her decision and is going with another company. Because you've invested time into her and have gotten to know her, you decide to ask if it would be OK to stay in periodic touch. Down the line, she may decide she's not happy with the company she chose and wants to change. Because you've stayed in touch with her and continued to invest in the relationship after being told no, you've positioned yourself to have a great opportunity to get the business.

Here's another example of how this can work in your favor. Let's say you're an event planner and you've been talking to the marketing manager of a commercial flooring company about their upcoming year-end customer appreciation event. After three months and multiple contacts, the company decides to hire the same event planner they've used for their past events. You've established a relationship with the marketing manager and therefore are staying in periodic touch. That manager has now moved to another flooring company but is able to contact you because your follow-up ensures she remembers you and has your contact information. The company she moved to has never had year-end customer appreciation parties and she's going to coordinate their first one. The owner of the new company wants her to get quotes from several event planners. You now have the opportunity to get that business—and a leg up on other event planners who don't already have an established relationship with the manager.

Scripting

"Joe, I understand your decision not to move forward and want to thank you for the time you've given me. If it's OK with you, I'd like to stay in periodic touch."

If you feel a connection, most likely the prospect does as well. Don't be afraid to ask for permission. The scripting is easy and respectful, and shows the prospect you're still interested in the relationship even though you've been told no.

Result #2

Develop Loyalty

We're going to focus on two types of loyalty in this section: customer loyalty and prospect loyalty.

Customer Loyalty

There's much common knowledge about customer loyalty. It's a key ingredient in customer retention. You may have heard that it takes far more time, energy and money to go get a new customer than it does to keep the ones you have. It's true. When you have customer loyalty, you will gain a level of comfort and confidence knowing that your customer base isn't vulnerable to be preyed on by your competition. The only way to create loyalty is to take care of your customers, and you do this by investing and showing appreciation. It's the only way to establish loyalty. Another benefit to taking care of your relationships is you'll always have a competitive advantage.

Loyalty doesn't live in the business; it lives in the relationship. It doesn't matter how good you are or how happy customers are with your product or service; that's just not enough to keep them loyal. Being good is expected. People aren't going to decide to do business with you if they think you might be less than good. Being good is par; there's nothing special about it. You've got to do more.

Being good is not a good enough reason for your customers to stay with you or remember you. Give them a better reason.

When I wrote my first book I had it made into an audio book. The company I used was good. The sales rep has always been nice and responsive, and has taken care of my orders with no problems. When it came time to place my last order, I couldn't remember the sales rep's name. She has never stayed in touch or reached out to me for any reason. I order my CDs in bulk so it had been about a year or so since my last order. I knew she had a very unique name and I still couldn't remember it. I had to go back to my last order to get it. If I turn *this* book into an audio version, I will shop around for quotes. There will be no reason not to. This rep has never invested a moment into me and therefore I have zero loyalty toward her. She's good; she delivered the product but that's what I expected when I decided to do business with her. She has done nothing beyond that to earn my loyalty.

This is the danger that occurs when you don't invest. I'm a recurring customer who she's at risk of losing. It appears she has taken my business for granted. I'm sure she has competitors that are equally as good and may even have better pricing. If she had my loyalty, I wouldn't shop around. Shopping around is going to take time and it certainly would be easier to stay with her company, but I'm not compelled to do so without checking out other companies. I want to reiterate, she is good, but that's just not enough. There's nothing special about it.

If you're in a transactional business, you're in more danger of losing customer loyalty if you're not staying in touch. Don't think, *"I've already done business with her so she won't need my services again."* This is foolish thinking. Customers may not need your services any time soon or possibly ever again, but they may know someone who will.

I also don't want you to be content thinking, *"my customer is happy with me and/or my product/service, so he'll remember me and remain loyal."* If customers don't hear from you consistently and know you care beyond business reasons, loyalty is hard to come by.

Appreciation is at the heart of loyalty, so showing appreciation to those who are important is paramount in getting their loyalty. Maya Angelou's famous quote is true: *"people will forget what you said, people will forget what you did, but people will never forget how you made them feel."* I believe the best way to have an effect on how someone feels is through appreciation. In Part II, I will share different ways you can show appreciation to your customers.

Prospect Loyalty

Now that you have a deeper understanding of customer loyalty, let's move on to prospect loyalty. This is very real and most people don't understand it.

I'm sure you'll agree with me that, in general, prospects don't buy in the first meeting or on the first phone call. When they don't, you enter what I call the holding pattern. The holding pattern is the time from when you meet the prospect until the time they buy. The holding pattern is where most people get discouraged. This is when multiple contacts take place and oftentimes it appears nothing is happening. However, the holding pattern is invaluable time for you to show prospects who you are, how you do business and how important they are to you. This is when you start earning credibility and trust. This is your time to shine, so when it comes time for prospects to make their decision, you've got their buy-in because of how you've handled the relationship. Take on the mindset to start treating your prospects like they're already customers.

If I meet a prospect who tells me she's interested in my services, but it's not a good time and she asks me to follow up in a month, I'm going to be excited about this. Of course, I would love for her to be ready in that first meeting, but we've already established that isn't too common. The reason I'm excited is because I now have the opportunity to start showing her who I am, how I do business and how important she is to me. I have systems in place that will support every action I need to take.

I was at an event and met a woman named Lauren who was VERY interested in my services. She was excited and couldn't wait to get started. To make a long story short, it took me 11 months and 17 contacts to get into her office for the first meeting. She told me she and her husband go over their schedules every day and after telling him she was meeting with me, he told her he knows someone who "does that" and she should meet with his person. She told him, *"I could never go with anyone but Wanda because she has been following up with me for a year."* I had invested well and created enough loyalty that she wouldn't even take a referral from her husband. I had only met her one time, but was able to establish a good enough relationship with her through the follow up process to earn her loyalty.

That is prospect loyalty at its best.

I want you to understand that follow-up doesn't have to be pushy. Over the course of the 11 months, I had contacted Lauren in different ways. I wasn't always asking if she was ready to move forward. That gets obnoxious and "stalkerish." Your contacts should always be a mixed bag of goods, which I'll discuss further in Chapter 6. My contacts with Lauren included a holiday card, birthday card, sharing additional information about my services and following up to get the first meeting booked. This kept the contacts interesting. She's one of my top customers. Don't give up, stay in the game.

Result #3

Become Referable

This is the grand prize from a prospecting point of view.

When you've put forth the necessary efforts that have resulted in strengthening your relationships and creating loyalty, you've now become referable. This doesn't just happen. You have to work at it, but it's some of the most important work you'll do. Referrals are the easiest leads you'll ever get. You've got somebody promoting you and your product and/or service. Your referral sources are comfortable referring you because you've proven your ability to take care of relationships and they're confident you'll handle their referrals in the same way you handle your relationship with them.

I'd venture to say that everyone in business would love to have lead generation be referral based. It cuts down on the time and cost to generate new business, while increasing your likelihood of making the sale. When you meet a prospect at an event, it takes time to get to know that person and more importantly, for that person to get to know you and your company, products or services. When a prospect is referred, most likely the referral source has given you an approval rating, so you're much further ahead in the process than you would be if you were dealing with a cold prospect.

When you receive a referral, it's critical to respond promptly and be sure to keep the referrer updated about the status of the referral. Have you ever given someone a referral and then wondered what happened? What's worse is to find out that a transaction took place. That's a terrible situation because it appears that the recipient of the referral is ungrateful and not being attentive to the "hand that fed her."

Keeping the referral source updated is a reflection of how well you're taking care of the referral, how you're continuing to show appreciation for it, and how you're remaining attentive to it. It also shows the referral source that you're not forgetting about him. This type of attention is reflective of how you handle your relationships. When a referral source gives you a referral, you are now a representation of that person. That's a responsibility that should be taken very seriously. Make the referral source look good.

A comment I hear frequently is, *"I'm not comfortable asking for referrals."* This immediately means one thing to me: there hasn't been enough invested into the relationship. When you invest well, you are comfortable asking for whatever you need. Relationships are like a bank account; you have to make some deposits before you can think about making a withdrawal.

I have a client named Dave who sells solar roofs. Before I started coaching Dave, he was already the #1 salesperson in the company. He was successful, knew what he was doing, obviously took the right actions and had some very strong habits developed. Dave impresses me in many ways and one of them is the fact that even though he was doing so well, he still knew there was opportunity for him to do even better. Oftentimes when we're doing well, we think, *"I'm good, what I'm doing is working."* This is true. What successful people are doing is working; otherwise they wouldn't be successful. However, there's always room for improvement. The most elite athletes in the world have coaches. They're already among the best, but they're always striving to be better.

When I started working with Dave, I realized his actions weren't completely systematized. We tightened them up and added a couple other actions to his following up and staying in touch system, and it wasn't long before his production increased.

"I have been a solar sales consultant for six years and I've never had a process for my follow-up. After just a few sessions

with Wanda, my follow-up process is completely dialed in, precise and automatic. My business has tripled in six months and I'm considering only taking referrals because I can't handle the increased lead volume. I'm not sure where I would be without Wanda's advice and attention to my specific situation."

— Dave Gersz, Solar PV Specialist, Stellar Solar

Selling solar roofs is a very transactional business. Many of Dave's customers are a one-time hit. Of course, there is the possibility his customers will buy another home or have multiple properties, but that's the exception rather than the rule. Having said that, Dave has built his lead generation to be nearly referral based. He shows us when you combine the right actions with good follow-up/stay-in-touch systems, the sky's the limit. Achieving this level of success is possible through the power of systems and good habits.

Numerous studies have been done that show the average person knows 250 people. Imagine if every person you know gave you two referrals. What would that do to your business?

I'm going to challenge you to write down 100 people you know on the list provided. Once the list is written, ask yourself if any of the people on it are potential customers or may know someone who could be a potential customer. If the answer is yes, the next question to ask yourself is, whether you've invested enough in the relationship to be comfortable asking for their business or a referral. If the answer is no, start investing. I'll teach you how to do that in Part II. I want you to realize that you already know people who can contribute to your success, and therein lies your goldmine.

You may be thinking you don't know 100 people, but I bet

you probably do. You just don't realize it. To help get you started with your list, think about the following:

- Contacts in your cell phone
- Contacts in your email
- Business cards sitting on your desk
- Contacts in other programs you have that house contact lists
- Existing customers
- Past customers
- Referral sources
- Your banker
- Your boss (current and past)
- Colleagues
- Your CPA
- Your financial planner
- Your insurance agent
- Your dentist
- Your hairstylist
- Your realtor
- College friends
- High school friends
- Neighbors

PEOPLE I KNOW

1. ____________________
2. ____________________
3. ____________________
4. ____________________
5. ____________________
6. ____________________
7. ____________________
8. ____________________
9. ____________________
10. ____________________
11. ____________________
12. ____________________
13. ____________________
14. ____________________
15. ____________________
16. ____________________
17. ____________________
18. ____________________
19. ____________________
20. ____________________
21. ____________________
22. ____________________
23. ____________________
24. ____________________
25. ____________________
26. ____________________

27. ______________________________
28. ______________________________
29. ______________________________
30. ______________________________
31. ______________________________
32. ______________________________
33. ______________________________
34. ______________________________
35. ______________________________
36. ______________________________
37. ______________________________
38. ______________________________
39. ______________________________
40. ______________________________
41. ______________________________
42. ______________________________
43. ______________________________
44. ______________________________
45. ______________________________
46. ______________________________
47. ______________________________
48. ______________________________
49. ______________________________
50. ______________________________
51. ______________________________
52. ______________________________
53. ______________________________

54. ______________________________
55. ______________________________
56. ______________________________
57. ______________________________
58. ______________________________
59. ______________________________
60. ______________________________
61. ______________________________
62. ______________________________
23. ______________________________
64. ______________________________
65. ______________________________
66. ______________________________
67. ______________________________
68. ______________________________
69. ______________________________
70. ______________________________
71. ______________________________
72. ______________________________
73. ______________________________
74. ______________________________
75. ______________________________
76. ______________________________
77. ______________________________
78. ______________________________
79. ______________________________
80. ______________________________

81. ______________________________
82. ______________________________
83. ______________________________
84. ______________________________
85. ______________________________
86. ______________________________
87. ______________________________
88. ______________________________
89. ______________________________
90. ______________________________
91. ______________________________
92. ______________________________
93. ______________________________
94. ______________________________
95. ______________________________
96. ______________________________
97. ______________________________
98. ______________________________
99. ______________________________
100. ______________________________

Once your list is complete, contact each person about doing business with you or ask for a referral. If you're not comfortable doing that, it's because you haven't invested enough—so your next step is to start that process. You'll learn how to do that in Part II.

The following story illustrates several of the points I've made thus far and will help you further understand the power of following up and staying in touch.

As mentioned earlier, I was a business banker for 25 years. The last bank I worked for was acquired and I was a Senior Vice President. When you're part of senior management and not with the lead bank in a merger, oftentimes you're no longer needed, which is the boat I was in. It was the first merger I ever experienced. I dodged that bullet for a very long time. It was 2009 and as you may remember, we were in one of the worst economic times on record. The misery really started in 2008 and I experienced enough of the turmoil from 2008 to 2009 to know that I didn't want to stay in the industry. Banking was in the middle of the economic firestorm and it wasn't something I wanted to be a part of any longer. I made the decision to become self-employed and give that a try. The million-dollar question was…self-employed in what?

As a banker, I frequently heard the following comments:

"You always call when you say you will."

"You always stay in touch."

"You never forget my birthday."

At the time, these comments didn't really mean much to me, but once I made the decision to become self-employed, I thought more about them. What was the intrigue and curiosity about how I did this?

I didn't think I was doing anything out of the ordinary. I set up some systems and followed them consistently. That was it, no magic or mystery to it. But I heard these comments enough to know something was there.

I decided to start speaking on the subject of follow-up and

share how I do it. I learned quickly that in general, people are not very good at follow-up, by their own admission. I'm always pleasantly surprised at the honesty that is conveyed to me. I realized I could make this a viable business. I started speaking to networking groups and business organizations, teaching workshops to sales teams, and providing individual coaching programs.

I also decided to become an independent sales rep for a greeting card company while I was building my follow-up business. The owner of the card company changed the pricing on the packages. He emailed all the reps on a Friday and told us to roll out the new pricing, he was going to challenge us to get five new customers the following week. One had to be the top package and the other four could be any of the other packages.

My immediate thought was, *"this should be easy."* How many prospects would it take to get five new customers—20, 50, 100, who knows? What I did know was I didn't have time to go get new prospects for this challenge. I didn't need to though because I have the habit of staying in periodic touch with some prospects who'd previously said no. I knew those were the people I would contact first. When I contacted them, I said, *"we have new pricing on the packages and I want to see if you'd be open to looking at the program again to see if it's a better fit."* It was a very easy and comfortable call for me to make. The reason it was easy was because I had stayed in touch. What would have made this call uncomfortable is if these people hadn't heard from me in six months, a year or longer. I didn't have that issue, and by the end of the week, I got my five new customers.

The owner emailed all us reps again on the Friday the challenge ended for the first week and told us he was going to put it out again: get five new customers next week. Same as in week

1, one had to be the top package and the other four could be any of the other packages. I dug deeper into my CRM of contacts and got my five customers. (I'll discuss CRM's in Part II).

The owner emailed us again on the Friday the second challenge ended and told us he was going to ask us to do it one more time. The story was the same: get five new customers the following week, one being the top package and the other four any of the other packages. This made the overall challenge to get 15 new customers in three weeks.

The challenge ended at 9 p.m. on Friday. It was 5 p.m. and I had my four customers at the lower packages, but still needed to get one at the top package. When you get good at follow-up, you'll be told no, you'll be ignored and you'll hear *"I'll think about it."* I went through a lot of noes, ignores and I'll think about its to get to my 14 yesses. Since it was so close to the deadline, I didn't have time for another no, ignore or I'll think about it. I also didn't have time to find someone who could use the card program. I needed to find someone who would be willing to do me a $500 favor. I had that person in mind and it was time to make the call. His name was Bill, a banking client of mine. One mistake I don't make is compartmentalizing my relationships based on what I do, or by project or transaction. If this is how you're basing your relationships, you're operating from a self-fulfilling mindset. I had invested a lot of time in Bill as a banker. I got to know his wife and his three kids became clients. At the point of this challenge, I'm 2 ½ years down the road out of banking. Bill no longer needed me and I no longer needed him. But, I liked Bill and just because I was no longer a banker wasn't a reason to stop investing in the relationship.

At 5:00 I called Bill. He answers and I tell him I've been in a challenge for three weeks and I'm one person away from hitting the mark. I asked him if he would be open to doing me a favor and getting the program to put me over the "finish line." He said yes, but asked me to call him back at 7:00 because he was at a wine tasting event. Of course I said I would. At 7:00 I called him and got his voicemail. I left a message: *"Hi Bill, this is Wanda. I'm calling you back. It's 7:00 and you thought this would be a good time to get you signed up for the program. Give me a call when you can; the challenge ends at 9:00."*

When you're calling prospects, you have to remind them why you're calling. Don't assume they'll remember. Make it easy on them.

Time was ticking away: 7:30, 8:00, 8:30 and no returned phone call. Remember earlier when I said one reason 90% of people quit after two contacts is because they make assumptions? This is a time when it would have been really easy to start assuming. The thoughts would look like this:

- He doesn't really want to get the program for me.
- He just said yes to be nice.
- He's at a wine tasting event and doesn't want to be bothered.

When you make assumptions, the phone can get very heavy. You can make assumptions that are so grand it will be impossible to pick up the phone because it will weigh 1,000 pounds.

I know not to make assumptions. The only thing I knew was he told me he would do it. By allowing only the facts into my thought process, it made the phone very easy to pick up.

I could have had another round of thoughts that looked like this:

- You tried Wanda. You called him twice; what more can you do?
- You should be proud of yourself; you got 14 new customers in three weeks. You were just one away from completing the challenge.
- You're tired. There's a lot of work involved in getting 14 new customers in three weeks. I'm not even talking about the prospecting part. Just servicing 14 new customers in that short timeframe was demanding. I was exhausted.

If you have these thoughts, what you're really doing is justifying not taking action to make yourself feel better. These thoughts will also keep you from having to do something that may be uncomfortable. But you have to be uncomfortable, because that's where growth happens. There's no room for growth in your comfort zone. If you allow justifying thoughts to prevent you from taking action, what you're really doing is preventing yourself from success.

Because I don't make assumptions or allow justifying thoughts to enter my mind, I easily picked up the phone at 8:30 and called Bill again. This time he answered. All I had to do was say, *"Hi Bill, this is Wanda."* He jumped in from there and said, *"I'm so sorry I haven't called you. I came back to the restaurant and it's been crazy busy."* At the time, he owned a restaurant and him going back there never would have been one of my assumptions. It was a Friday night so of course that's a busy time for restaurants. He then said, *"so what do you need?"* I told him I needed his credit card information and in two minutes we were done. It was no big deal to him, but do you see how I could have made it a big deal with my assumptions.

I was telling this story at an event and a gentleman came up to me afterward. He said it was easy for me to ask for Bill's credit card information because I'm a woman. I told him I didn't ask for Bill's credit card information; he asked me what I needed and I told him his credit card information. Then this gentleman went on to say that was easy for me to do because I had a good relationship with Bill. I told him that was my point. If you have good relationships and you invest wisely, you can comfortably ask for whatever you need. As the man walked away, I actually felt bad for him. I was of the impression that he was looking for reasons to justify why that happened for me and couldn't happen for him. Do you ever do that? Hear about someone's success and then start justifying why they could achieve it, but you couldn't? If you do, I'm going to ask you to stop it. You can do whatever you want if you're willing to establish the habits and disciplines that will support the success you desire.

I found out the next week that out of over 100,000 reps in U.S., Canada and Australia, only 15 hit the challenge for all three weeks. We received a lot of local and national recognition. We were recognized at the annual convention and when we were on stage, I was looking at an audience of over 3,000 people. That moment changed my life. I felt in my heart of hearts that there should be 3,000 people on stage and 15 in the audience. I felt very strongly about this because completing this challenge wasn't hard. It did take a lot of work, but that's different than it being difficult. All the other reps needed to meet this challenge was to have good follow-up and stay- in-touch systems in place that create strong relationships. It was then that I realized and felt I had a responsibility to take my follow-up business much more seriously. It put me on a mission to help everyone I can implement effective follow-up systems so they can easily build their businesses and strengthen their relationships.

Had I not been willing to make that third phone call to Bill I wouldn't have made it on that stage, which means I wouldn't be writing this book or speaking and coaching at the level I am. You have no idea what success is waiting for you on the other side of that phone call, email, lunch, text, etc. Don't let your thoughts sell you short.

Result #4

Get More Opportunities

A big part of the reason why opportunities are lost in the sales world is because there's such a lack of follow-up. When you learn how to stay the course with a prospect and are willing to remain in the game regardless of how long it takes, it's impossible to not have a chance at every opportunity that comes your way. You may not get every opportunity, but you are sure to be one of the players in the game because you're in the elite 10% who make more than three contacts. If you quit after two contacts you're guaranteed to miss out on opportunities because you'll be pulling yourself out of the game.

Result #5

Develop a Robust Pipeline

You will say goodbye to thin pipelines with your *Follow Up Sales Strategies Systems* in place. The reason for this is because you will no longer lose track of your prospects. When a prospect tells you to follow up next week, month, or year, you'll have a system that won't let you forget about him, which increases your opportunity for more sales. If you only have a handful of prospects and two of them decide not to move forward with you in the same week, that hurts. When you have a robust pipeline, you don't feel the losses as much.

Result #6

Get More Sales

Your sales will increase because of your robust pipeline. As I've said, prospects are opportunities, so the bigger the pipeline, the more opportunities you have, which means you'll have higher odds for customer conversion. Sales is a numbers game.

Result #7

Get More Income

It's important that you like what you do and feel good about what you do and even better if what you do gives you purpose and passion. In addition to all that, you also want to make money. In the words of Zig Ziglar: *"if you tell me money isn't important, I'd have to believe you'd lie to me about anything."* Money is important. It gives you peace of mind, options, opportunity and the ability to give back. When you have strong relationships, create loyalty, are referable and have a robust pipeline that turns into more sales, your business will be money in the bank.

Result #8

Achieve Your Goals

Whether you work for someone or you're self-employed, I'm sure you have sales and income goals. When you're taking advantage of the opportunities you have and are systematically following up, you are far more likely to achieve your goals. When there isn't order and structure with your follow-up efforts, your practices will be haphazard and inconsistent which results in being ineffective. If you're not consistently doing the follow-up work, you won't be well supported in achieving your goals.

Result #9

Gain Consistency

Consistency is what will change your business. It creates credibility and trust, and makes you reliable and dependable. You can be counted on when you're consistent, and being in the flow of consistency is a confidence booster. You'll have great energy about you because you're consistently getting your follow-up work done, which means you're consistently working on building your business and strengthening your relationships. That's very empowering.

On the flip side, some examples of how inconsistency will prevent you from achieving success are presented as follows.

Let's say you've decided to lose weight and you get a membership to a local gym.

Week 1 – You got to the gym four times.

Week 2 – You got to the gym once.

Week 3 – You got to the gym twice.

Week 4 – You didn't get to the gym at all.

Can you see how this inconsistent action won't support your weight-loss goal?

Let's look at it from a follow-up perspective. In the *Follow Up Sales Strategies System*, you allocate time every working day to get your follow-up work done. This is discussed in detail in Part II.

Let's say you've set a goal to commit to your daily follow up time to get your follow-up work done.

Week 1 – On four days you got your scheduled follow-up work done.

Week 2 – On one day you got your scheduled follow-up work done.

Week 3 – On two days you got your scheduled follow-up work done.

Week 4 – You didn't get your follow-up work done at all.

This sort of inconsistency is what's going to create holes in your pipeline and weaken your relationships. Consistency is a must and is what will get you to the next level.

Result #10

Become Strategic

When you implement the *Follow Up Sales Strategies System*, you become very strategic. Your practices will be systematized and streamlined, and you will have laser focus. When your practices are strategic, you don't waste time and you get this important work done on a daily basis.

Result #11

Become Responsive

As you'll learn in Part II, with the *Follow Up Sales Strategies System*, you'll always be responsive to new contacts, prospects and existing customers. How quickly you respond creates trust. This system makes you aware of when action needs to be taken; you have allocated time for your follow-up work and you never forget about anyone. Believe me when I say, it's impossible to forget. You'll learn why that is later.

Result #12

Get Noticed/Stand Out

Because so many struggle in the area of following up and staying in touch, it's very easy to get noticed when you do. You're the exception who is attentive, follows through and doesn't give up. These are admirable traits that will get you noticed and make you stand out from the crowd.

Chapter 6
Consistently Stay in Touch

I'm hoping you now understand how critical it is to stay in touch. It doesn't have to be an arduous task that wears you out at the mere thought of doing it. Your savior in making this very manageable is your CRM, discussed in Chapter 7. I can't say this enough: you can't have a strong relationship with someone if you're not staying in consistent touch. Staying in touch will do many things including reminding recipients you're still in business. As much as you want to believe you'll be remembered, you may not if you're not staying in touch.

Strengthen Your Relationships

You'll see that when you stay in consistent touch, it won't always be about your business. Making contacts that are only about you and your business is very self-serving and can be a turnoff. You won't be creating any loyalty when your outreach is always about you. Think about the people who only contact you when they need something. It's not impressive. Strong relationships are well balanced.

Keep Your Tool Box Interesting

You want to make sure that how you're staying in touch is not the same every time. You must keep it interesting so recipients don't get bored or become numb to whatever it is you're sending. The following are the must-haves for your follow-up toolbox. The items aren't in any order of importance, but I'm starting with the digital tools since we live in such an electronic world.

- Social media
- Email
- Newsletters
- Cards
- Phone
- In-person get-together

Let's talk about each one individually.

Social Media

Social media sites are great tools for staying in touch. They help people remember you, but also provide the opportunity to learn about what's going on with those to whom you're connected. For instance, if you're on LinkedIn, you receive posts when someone is having a work anniversary or has changed positions or companies. Don't just mindlessly read them; see if there's a relationship or business-building opportunity that spurs you to contact the person, referencing the posting.

If you're not connected to someone that's important to you, send a request for a connection.

Email

Email is overused today. We are inundated with emails; who doesn't have a full inbox? I caution you to be careful about how you use email when following up and staying in touch. Email should be a backup for your follow-up work. In the *Follow Up Sales Strategies System*, you call first, then email. I'll discuss the logic for this process in Part II.

Be cognizant of why you're sending an email. Before hitting "send," ask yourself:

- Am I sending this email because it's convenient for me?
- Would it be easier for the recipient if I talked to him about this matter?
- Could this be resolved quicker with verbal communication?
- Is this a cumbersome email that will result in a deferred response?

Don't send unnecessary emails.

You also want to make sure you're not hiding behind your email. As already mentioned, when you follow up, you open yourself up to rejection. For this reason, many aren't comfortable using the phone, so they'll send an email with the justification that "it's quicker that way." Don't use email as a crutch. It's easier to be rejected or ignored over an email than it is on the phone—but you're going to have to develop your follow-up muscle and thicken your skin so the noes on the ever-so-important road to success doesn't stop you from taking effective action.

Other Ways to Effectively Use Email for Staying In Touch

When your emails are used for staying in touch contacts, it's important they're not in newsletter format. It's more personal when an email is addressed to one recipient rather than part of an email blast. For instance, personal emails can be used to send:

- Industry tips
- Something of interest to the recipient that doesn't have anything to do with your business
- A testimonial you recently received
- A video or a podcast link that will be of interest to the recipient

Newsletters

Newsletters are a great way to remind the recipient about you and your business. I was talking to a rep from a well-known marketing newsletter company who told me their studies show that a 20% open rate is good. This means that 80% of people receiving your newsletter are hitting delete, which isn't necessarily a bad thing. Yes, it would be best if they read your newsletter, but if they don't, at least they're being reminded of you and your business.

I strongly suggest you get people's permission before adding them to your distribution list. They may or may not be interested in your newsletter and to simply add them to your mailing list is quite presumptuous and can be irritating (and is frowned upon per online communication protocol.)

While electronic tools are great, they will never replace human interaction. Here's a quote that might help put this into perspective:

> *"It is appallingly obvious that technology has exceeded our humanity."*
>
> — Albert Einstein, 1879-1955

If Albert Einstein felt this way in the '50s, can you imagine what he would think today? I believe he'd be appalled beyond words. I'm in no way knocking electronic tools or technology; they're incredible and we can do so much with them. My point is you shouldn't rely on them as your sole means of communication. Electronic tools will suffice, but they won't set you apart.

Now, let's talk about some tools that are often considered old-fashioned.

Handwritten Note/Card

Sending a handwritten note is a lost art. Because of that, it's easy to stand out and be different by simply putting pen to paper. Because so few do this, it will be a pleasant surprise to the recipient. Following are some reasons to send a handwritten note/card. And by the way, I'm talking about sending these cards "snail mail," the old-fashioned way.

- Business anniversary
- Birthday
- Holidays
- Nice to meet you
- Thank you for your business, referral, time or opportunity

Phone

The phone is the most effective tool we have. It's a huge time saver and it creates human interaction. Some reasons to use the phone are:

- Business anniversary
- Birthday
- Checking in to see how they're doing with your product or service

- Just because (This call is NOT about business. You're merely calling to say hi and see how the person is doing.)
- Thank you for your business, referral, time or opportunity

Have you heard anyone say, "the money is in the call"? It is.

In-Person Get-Together

I bet there are people within your contacts who are worthy of your time. There's nothing better and more effective in relationship building than spending time with someone. Who you decide to spend time with will depend on the relationship, the size of business transacted and your budget. If there are people with whom you know you should be spending more time, but you have budget constraints, get creative. Following are some ideas on how you can spend time with those who are important to you and deserving of your time.

Coffee

There is a coffee house on just about every corner, so this is something that's easy to do and pretty easy on your wallet. If you feel coffee drinks are too expensive, get a $2 cup of tea instead. This is a very cost-effective way to spend time with someone.

Lunch/Dinner

I can pretty much guarantee that you have contacts who will respond positively to having lunch or dinner with you. If budget is a factor, there are all-you-can-eat buffets, delis, and mom and pop restaurants that are quite affordable. It doesn't have to be fancy. You won't be judged on the location; you'll be praised for wanting to spend time with the person you've invited. Another approach is to not treat and just send an invitation to get together for lunch with no intention of picking up the bill. This works perfectly well. It's about spending time with the person and not about whether you treat or not. I don't want any excuses to come up in your mind as to why you can't make this all-important gesture.

Another angle on lunch is to bring it in to the person's office for the staff. This is always a big hit. You can do it Lunch-n-Learn style or just keep it social.

Sporting Event

There are two ways you can go on this. If you have a customer who is a football fan and you get tickets to a game, you can either give the tickets to him or invite him to go with you.

Other sports outings that involve actual participation—not just watching—are playing a round of golf, tennis or any other activity you have in common.

When you're following up and staying in touch with these tools, you're investing wisely into your relationships. This is how you show appreciation, which will turn into loyalty.

As I close Part I, I hope you have a new perspective on how much depth there is to follow-up. That it goes way beyond the prospecting stage and why it's critical to stay in touch after the sale has been closed. I'm also hopeful that you can clearly see how much following up and staying in touch can increase your business and strengthen your relationships.

I need you to really understand everything you've read so far. It's this understanding that will keep you committed to implementing and consistently using the *Follow Up Sales Strategies System*. If you're ready, let's get started.

PART II

IMPLEMENTING THE FOLLOW UP SALES STRATEGIES SYSTEM

I want to point out again that everything you've learned so far and what you're about to learn is nothing more than a habit. You have to be willing to stay committed until the habit is developed. Implementing the *Follow Up Sales Strategies System* will have a significant impact on the way you do business and it will change your life if you let it.

Chapter 7
Get Organized With a System

At the heart of a good follow-up system is a Customer Relationship Manager (CRM) / database program / contact management system, which all mean the same thing. For the purpose of this book, I will use the term CRM.

You can't be really good at follow-up if you're not using a CRM. All the other systems I mentioned that don't work—spiral notebooks, sticky notes, email, Word or Excel, and your head—can be replaced by a CRM. If you don't know what a CRM is, in its simplest form, it's your program that tells you who needs to be contacted and when. It's your assistant who never forgets anything. It holds the contact information for those who are important to you, i.e., name, address, email, website, etc.; it has task reminder dates to notify you when you need to take action on someone; and it has a notes section where you document all your actions.

A comment I hear frequently is, *"I'm not good at follow-up because I'm not organized."* If this is you, I have good news. You don't have to be an organized person to get your follow-up work done. You just have to be willing to use your CRM. It will organize you.

One of the main problems with disorganization is it's a

time killer. When you're organized, you don't waste time on nonsense such as sifting through piles of paper, trying to find contact information for someone you need to call or trying to remember previous conversations. Using the three components of your CRM discussed in the next chapter will rid you from suffering through unorganized chaos.

According to Thesauras.com, synonyms for unorganized are:

- All over the place
- Chaotic
- Cluttered
- Confused
- Messy
- Scattered

None of these words are very becoming.

If you appear to be unorganized, you run the risk of your customers, prospects, referral sources and anyone else perceiving you in any one of these negative ways.

On the flip side, according to Thesauras.com, one of the synonyms of organized is:

- Systematized

This one word encapsulates the point of this entire book. Your follow-up efforts must be systematized to be effective. All your systems are centered in your CRM, which is why it will organize you.

Using your CRM is nothing more than a habit. When you experience how powerful it is, you won't consider not using it.

With today's technology, CRMs can have a lot of bells and whistles that can be intimidating, especially if you're not a techie. It's important that the program you choose is user-friendly. If it's too difficult and cumbersome, you won't use it.

There are hundreds of CRM programs available. I suggest you Google CRMs and research a few at a time. Don't research too many because it will get confusing. They all generally offer the same features, just in different ways. It's important to find the one that works for you.

Most programs have monthly fees generally ranging from $7 to $200. Be open to paying the fee. As I said earlier, the program is your assistant who never forgets anything. How much is that worth? Your CRM is one of your most valuable assets. It's where you house your goldmine. You can't put a price tag on that, so don't be penny-wise and pound-foolish.

Other questions you may have when you're doing your research:

- What are the maximum contacts allowed?
- Can I import my contacts from Excel?
- Does the program sync with Outlook or other programs that are important to you?
- Is there an app for the program?
- Do they have a customer service department?

Find a program that works best for you, implement it and use it without fail. Whatever system you use, be sure you consistently update it and make it your #1 follow-up tool. You can have the best program in existence, but if you don't develop a habit of using it, it doesn't do you any good.

If you already have a CRM, go through the contact list and make sure the information for each person is current. Get rid of any contacts who are no longer good or ones with whom you don't want to stay in touch. Having a clean and up-to-date contact list is an important part of getting organized. You want the relationships in your CRM to be meaningful and those you want to focus on and invest in.

Keep It Simple

There are only three components to a CRM that you really need.

Component #1
Web-Based

It's best to find a program that's web-based rather than software on your computer. When it's web-based, you'll have access to it wherever you are.

Component #2
Multiple Reminder/Task Dates

It's important you have the option for multiple reminder/ task dates. Some programs' terminology is reminder date and others is task. For the purpose of this book, I'm going to use the term reminder date. You'll have multiple reasons to follow up/stay in touch with a contact and having multiple reminder dates allows you to do this with ease. For example, let's say I have a customer whose birthday is June 11. I have a reminder date set for that day. In October, this customer contacts me and tells me she has a friend who is a sales manager and is interested in my workshop for his sales team. My customer is having lunch with her friend next Wednesday and wants me to follow up with her on Thursday, which will be October 21. I'll set a reminder date for that day. I now have two reminder dates for her, one for her birthday and one to follow up regarding her referral. If the CRM only allows one reminder date per contact, it can become confusing.

The reminder date is your call to action for each contact.

You'll want to find out what happens to past due reminders. If you weren't able to get to a reminder yesterday, where will it show up today? Some systems will flag the past due reminders in a different color or tag them in a different way than the reminders for the current day. This is very important to find out because this how you don't lose track or forget about someone you were supposed to contact.

Component #3

Notes Section

Having a good notes section is crucial to a good system. You will document all conversations, contacts and communications in the notes section for each contact. This will rid you of all those other systems that don't work that I discussed earlier. Think of it as downloading or dumping into the notes section.

If you're thinking you don't have time to document every contact, conversation and communication, I want you to clear your head of that thought. You have to make the time to do this and I'm going to teach you how. If a prospect tells you to follow up in one month and you do so, how are you going to remember what was said? Are you going to have to sift through pages of notes from a month ago, dig into your memory bank so deep that it hurts, or look through old sticky notes or deleted emails? All these scenarios are stressful and big time wasters.

In addition, you open yourself up to potential embarrassment with the prospect because you're not going to fully remember what was said. You can eliminate all this stress by simply using the notes section. Everything I'm teaching you is going to save you time. I just need you to trust the process and be willing to develop the new habits.

When you decide on a program, all you need to do is learn how to input contacts, attach reminder dates and document in the notes section. That is not intimidating at all. If this is all you know how to do with the program you've chosen, you are good to go and on your way to becoming exceptional at follow-up.

When getting your CRM up and running, your first task at hand will be inputting your contacts into the program. There are two ways to do this:

1. Manually
2. Import from Excel

Regarding #2, most programs have an import/export feature. Once you get your contacts into an Excel spreadsheet, this is a good time to "scrub" the list before importing. You want to make sure the contacts going in are meaningful. How you determine that is ask yourself if this is a relationship I want to invest in. If the answer is yes, put them in.

The second task at hand is getting reminder dates attached to each contact. As mentioned earlier, the reminder date is your call to action. Having your contacts in the CRM with no reminder date attached is no different than having a business card sitting on your desk. Later, I'll teach you how to determine what the contact date should be.

I want to mention one other part of the CRM implementation.

You will experience a degree of frustration because you're learning a new program. Don't let this get in your way. Recognize it and remind yourself this is nothing more than a learning curve and as soon as you understand the program in the simple way you need to, the frustration will be gone. One approach is to spend secluded time getting familiar with the program. Again, all you need to learn is how to input contacts, set reminders and use the notes section.

Avoid Overwhelm by Using Your System

What creates overwhelm:

- Feeling unorganized
- Not following up when you say you will
- Not staying in touch the way you should
- Knowing you're losing business because you're not following up

I promise you all of this will go away if you will commit to using your CRM on a daily basis.

Have your CRM up while you're at your desk. You don't want to waste time having to log in every time you need it. Ideally, you should be in and out of the program throughout the day because you're talking to prospects, customers, and referral sources. You'll be updating the notes section and advancing the reminder dates after each conversation.

Never Lose Track of Your Relationships Again

It's impossible to forget about someone when they're in your CRM because you have a reminder date attached to every contact. You're notified as to when it's time to reach out. And if you aren't able to make the contact on the scheduled day, it will be impossible to forget about because the reminder will be flagged as past due. The reminder date is what allows you to follow up and consistently stay in touch with ease, preventing you from ever losing track of anyone.

I always get accolades about how good I am at follow-up. But the truth is, it's not follow-up that I'm good at. What I'm good at is using my CRM. It allows me to be responsive, impressionable and known as the kind of person who takes care of my relationships.

Once you have your CRM up and running, you'll then build systems and timelines within it.

Do Systems Really Work?

Absolutely! I've heard many people say they're not "systems people". They prefer to go with the flow and follow up when it feels right or when time permits. This is a "hang loose" attitude and approach toward something that plays a critical part in allowing you to consistently get this very important work done—work that needs daily attention. These same people think systems are too rigid, boring and inflexible.

If you don't feel you're a systems person, I hope I can change your perspective. Systems are nothing more than organized actions toward a desired result. They create boundaries, timelines and structure. They help you form habits. They will become your best friend. Not operating in a systematized fashion opens the door for disorder, chaos and confusion.

Let's look at another interpretation of systems:

Save
Your
Self
Time
Energy
Money

That's exactly what systems do; they save you time, energy and money. Now are you on board?

Once your CRM is set up, it's time to start implementing your systems. They don't have to be complicated or difficult, because if they are, you won't stay with them. Thus, allow me to simplify things for you, which will increase your commitment to the process.

System #1

Schedule Your Follow-up Time

I'm going to ask you to schedule your follow-up time on a weekly basis. Decide on what day of the week you're going to schedule your follow-up time for the upcoming week. Friday can be a good day for scheduling. I want you to calendar 30 minutes a day for follow-up for the upcoming week. This time will be scheduled on working days only. Schedule the time as early in the day as possible, but not so early that you can't make calls. The earlier in the day the time is scheduled, the less chance the day has of taking over. I'm sure your schedule varies, so one day as early as possible may be 9:00 a.m. and on another day it may not be until 2:30 p.m. This doesn't matter. What's important is that you have your follow-up time on your calendar. I want you to treat this time as a non-negotiable commitment. It should have the same priority as a meeting with a prospect or customer.

Getting your follow-up time in every workday is nothing more than a habit. We're not perfect when forming new habits, so if you miss a day, don't try to make up for the lost time. Just "get back on the horse" the following day. Determine why you missed the day and figure out how to ensure it doesn't happen again. I also don't want you to stack the time. In other words, if you look at your calendar for the upcoming week, and you have a full schedule on Tuesday and Wednesday, don't think, "I'll just schedule 1 ½ hours on Thursday" (30 minutes for each day). If something unforeseen happens on Thursday and you weren't able to get to your follow-up time, you've now gone three days with no follow-up. What's critical is developing the daily habit.

Set up a contact in your CRM for the weekly scheduling. The first name field could be Schedule and the last name field could be Follow-Up Time. Then set a reminder date for the upcoming Friday. When you get your time scheduled, advance the reminder date to the following Friday. This way, you don't have to try to remember it's Friday and you need to schedule your follow-up time, because your CRM will tell you. If Fridays don't work, choose the day that's best for you.

I want to talk about working on your business versus working in your business. When you're working in your business, you're in essence servicing your clientele. When you're working on your business, you're building your business and strengthening your relationships. When you're in follow-up time, you're working on your business. Regardless of how busy you are working in your business, you can't use this as a reason not to get in your daily follow-up time. Ideally, you want to always be busy with in your business work and the more you build, the busier you'll be, but it should never be at the expense of your follow-up time. The danger of spending the majority of your time working in your business is when that business is transacted, you'll more than likely be looking at a thin pipeline because you've been spending your time in your business and not on your business. Having scheduled daily follow-up time allows you to consistently work on your business without neglect, which will support your future growth.

Action steps:

1. Decide what day of the week you'll schedule your follow-up time for the upcoming week.
2. Set up a contact in your CRM for the weekly scheduling.
3. Schedule your follow-up time for the upcoming week.

Now that you have your follow-up time scheduled, you may be thinking, now what? Next up, we're going to systematize your follow-up work. It's important that it's systematized in the order of priority that follows. Doing so will save you time so you don't have to think about what to work on during your scheduled follow-up time. Thinking wastes time.

System #2

Daily Follow-up Work

1. Take care of your new contacts from the previous day, which includes inputting their contact information in your CRM, documenting the conversation/action to be taken in the notes section and setting up a reminder date.
2. Work on reminders for the current day.
3. Handle admin work, i.e., sending out cards, mailers,

marketing pieces, etc.

This work will build your business and strengthen your relationships on a daily basis.

If you will follow this order of 1, 2, 3, you will get all your follow-up work done. Nothing or no one will slip through the cracks. This 1, 2, 3-step process is your daily follow-up action plan.

You'll be so liberated when this work is getting done on a daily basis. One of the best reasons to do it as early in the day as possible is that once this work is done, the rest of the day is yours to enjoy. I don't mean go to the beach or play golf; I'm talking about being able to enjoy whatever else needs to be done and being present in all you do for the balance of the day. So many people have lost their joy in what they're doing because they're running crazy and carrying the follow-up boulder on their shoulder with them everywhere they go. Can you see how getting steps 1, 2 and 3 done every workday will lighten your load? Once you experience this feeling, you won't go back to the life of craziness, disorganization and chaos.

Mindset Shifts

As you allocate 30 minutes for daily follow-up and start developing this habit, your old ways of thinking are going to put unnecessary pressure on you with the following thoughts:

- I don't have time to do this.
- I should be doing something else.
- There's something more urgent that needs my attention.

These thoughts are nothing more than resistance in developing the new habits. When they enter your mind, replace them with:

- I allocate daily follow-up time to work "on" my business.
- Follow-up time supports my prospecting efforts.
- Daily follow-up time is necessary to build my business and relationships.
- Just 30 minutes is not going to make or break my day.
- The best thing I can do for the future success of my business is commit to my daily follow-up time.

Getting your daily follow-up work done is crucial. If this habit isn't formed, you're going to lose business and jeopardize relationships. You can't implement anything I've taught and will teach in the remainder of this book if you're not getting in your follow-up time. If you're struggling with this, use the following Daily Tracker to help you review the reasons why you're not getting in the time. This a good self-assessment tool that will help you detect patterns for why you're not honoring this very important time and allowing it into your schedule. I've said numerous times that you have to be committed. Stay on track.

Daily Follow-up Work Tracker

Date	30 Minutes Completed (Yes or No)	If Not, Why?

If nothing changes...then nothing changes!

Create Timelines That Will Support Consistent Action

As I've said before, consistency is what will change your business. If you don't have timelines and systems to keep you on track, your efforts will become haphazard. In other words, you'll be operating in an inconsistent manner—and when something is inconsistent, it becomes ineffective.

Keep the Follow-up Ball in Your Court at All Times

You have to understand the importance of having a follow-up conversation every time you talk to a prospect. In Chapter 3, I talked about follow-up emotions that are created by our thoughts and I promised to give you a tactic to keep these emotional thoughts at bay. The tactic is the follow-up conversation. Every one of these emotional thoughts has a common denominator and that is uncertainty. When you have follow-up conversations, you will eliminate uncertainty, which will get rid of these emotional thoughts.

I don't know if I should follow up.

I'm not sure if the prospect is interested.

I feel like I'm bothering the prospect.

I don't want to be a pest.

I don't want the prospect to think I'm a stalker.

You already know that in general, prospects don't buy in the first meeting or on the first phone call. They will usually tell you why. The reason may be because they need to think about it, go over their budget, talk to their boss or spouse, are waiting to hear back from your competitor or any other host of reasons that keep them from moving forward in that first contact. You can NEVER leave a meeting or hang up the phone without having the follow-up conversation. By having this conversation, you're keeping the ball in your court. You don't ever want it to be in the prospect's court. You want to be in control. One of the reasons you follow up is to build your business. If you're leaving the follow-up ball in the prospect's court, you're putting the future growth of your business in the prospect's hands. Not a good move.

Follow-up Conversation Scripting

When prospects tell you they're not ready to move forward, the conversation should go as follows:

You: *Sue, I certainly understand you wanting to go over your budget. Would it be OK if I followed up with you?*

Sue: *Of course.*

You: *Great, when would be a good time?*

Sue: *I should have my decision made by next Thursday.*

You: *I'll mark my calendar to follow up with you next Thursday.*

After the conversation, you're going to go into your CRM, document the date of the conversation and what was said then change the reminder date to next Thursday. You're done with Sue and don't have to think about her again until next Thursday, when the reminder shows up on your CRM.

If a prospect says she'll get back to you, the conversation should look like this:

You: *Sue, I certainly understand you wanting to go over your budget. Would it be OK if I followed up with you?*

Sue: *That's OK. I'll get back to you.*

You: *If for some reason I don't hear from you, would it be OK if I followed up?*

Sue: *That would be fine.*

You: *Great, when would be a good time?*

Sue: *I should have my decision made by next Thursday.*

You: *I'll mark my calendar to follow up with you next Thursday.*

What is paramount in the follow up conversation is you always ask when would be a good time. If you ask if you can follow up and the prospect says yes and you don't ask when, you're going to leave the meeting or hang up the phone with a question mark in your head...*when should I follow up?* When there are questions, it opens up the door for uncertainty, which brings about the negative thoughts that creates the follow up emotion which can stop you from taking action.

A comment I hear from some of my clients is, *"If a prospect says she'll get back to me, I'm not comfortable saying if for some reason I don't hear from you, would it be ok if I followed up."* There's no reason to be uncomfortable; I've never offended anyone with this question. In fact, I usually hear relief in their voice because I've just relieved them of the responsibility of having to get back to me. If you're uncomfortable asking this question, do it anyway. Remember, there's no room for growth in your comfort zone. You have to stretch yourself. Look at it like this, the worst that will happen is you'll hear no. You've done what you can, so you'll have to wait to hear from her—but that doesn't mean you should never follow up with her again. You would be remiss if you didn't follow up at least one more time. Are you thinking, *"she said she'd get back to me. Why*

would I follow up?" The answer is simple: it never hurts to try if you haven't heard back. For all you know, she'll be pleased you called because she meant to call you, but just hasn't had a chance.

You may have the follow-up conversation many times before you get the business. That doesn't matter. What matters is that you're always in control of the next follow-up step.

The follow-up emotion, "I feel like I'm bothering the prospect," feeds the discomfort of using the phone. To combat this, when you call and the prospect answers, identify yourself and then always ask if he has a minute. If he doesn't, he'll tell you. Don't take it personally if he says he doesn't have a minute. Appreciate his honesty. You don't want to talk to him if he's in the middle of a project, on his way out the door or under a deadline. He'll be distracted and it won't be an effective conversation. If he tells you he doesn't have time, follow up by asking if it would be OK to call him later. He'll say yes and then ask what time would be good. Do you see how this conversation should take place under all circumstances when talking to a prospect? If he wants you to call back on another day, update the notes section in your CRM and advance the reminder date to the day you're supposed to call back. Again, you won't have to think about the prospect again until you're notified by your CRM that it's time to make contact.

You're now going to implement System #3, which will support your follow-up efforts when you're in the prospecting phase. It doesn't matter who the prospect is, this system is what will keep you in the game. It will be impossible for you to forget about the prospect and equally as important, it will be impossible for the prospect to forget about you.

A big struggle for people is they don't know how to track or what to do when multiple contacts need to be made with a prospect. That's why 90% quit after two contacts. This system will put you in the elite 10% who make three contacts or more.

System #3

Prospecting Timeline

You'll see that I'm going to ask you to call your prospects and follow up with an email or text if you have to leave a voicemail. The logic behind this is as follows:

- When you call, the prospect will hear the sincerity and interest in your voice. She won't get this in an email or text.
- The phone is the most efficient tool you have. If you are fortunate enough to get her on the phone, what you can cover in a three-minute conversation can take multiple emails or texts and a number of days. You'll also be able to hear her level of interest by the tone of her voice. You won't get this in an email or text.
- Some people will respond quicker to emails or texts than they will to phone calls. Also, it's likely the prospect will keep your email in her inbox or text on her phone until she gets back to you. This way it's harder for her to forget about you. As you know, a voicemail message can be deleted once it's heard and then it's out of sight, out of mind. BUT she's hearing your voice—and that's reason alone to make the call.

If you're not used to making phone calls when you start this system, you may think, *"don't answer, don't answer."* This is normal in the beginning because it may be uncomfortable, but remember you can't grow in your comfort zone. The more you start using the phone, the more comfortable you'll get and your thought will change to, *"answer the phone, answer the phone."* You'll want people to answer the phone so you won't have to send an email or text, which will save you time.

Another resisting comment I get from my clients when I'm introducing this system is, *"I don't have time to make calls."* You'll learn that this is hogwash. If you make 10 calls, you might get two people who answer. How long does it take to leave a message? Maybe 30 seconds. It doesn't take any time at all to make calls. Thinking you don't have time is immediate mindset thinking and feeds resistance to forming the new habit.

What's the million dollar question I always get when it comes time to making multiple contacts? *"How do I know when to stop following up?"* My response is give it at least a year. You may be thinking *"whaaaaat,"* but hold on; you're going to see how easy that is with the following system.

As mentioned, when following up with prospects, you'll call first then send an email or text if you were unable to talk to the person. In the email, you'll let the prospect know you left a voicemail and follow up with the same message in writing

Scripting

Voicemail

Hi Joe, this is Wanda. We met last week at the chamber event. You were interested in my coaching services and asked me to follow up with you today. Give me a call when you get a moment and we can discuss your needs in further detail to see how I can support you. I look forward to hearing from you.

Email/Text

Hi Joe, I left you a voicemail and thought I would also email. We met last week at the chamber event. You were interested in my coaching services and asked me to follow up with you today. Give me a call when you get a moment and we can discuss your needs in further detail to see how I can support you. I look forward to hearing from you.

If you're sending a text, let Joe know who you are. Don't assume he's going to recognize your number or have it registered as a contact in his phone.

I talk to people on a daily basis about their follow up habits and the same two questions come up time and time again; *how often should I follow up and when should I stop following up.* I've created this timeline that will eliminate these questions from your thought process. It doesn't matter how many times you follow up. If you want to stay in the game and continue to stay in touch when you're being ignored, the following timeline is your answer.

The timeline is for when prospects are not getting back to you.

Initial call and email/text

Follow up one week later with a call and email/text

Follow up two weeks later with a call and email/text

Follow up one month later with a call and email/text

Follow up/stay in touch every three months

See how you're starting to back up a little bit with each contact. This keeps it respectful.

The initial, one week, two week and one-month contacts will

be about doing business with you. If you get out to the three-month contact, in addition to pursuing the business, you'll also start mixing up the contacts, i.e., newsletter, birthday, social media connections, holiday, etc. As I said earlier, this will keep it interesting and prevent you from being "stalkerish."

Every contact will be documented in the notes section. You'll document the action you took and advance the reminder date to the next contact date. Do you see how simple this is? With this system in place, following up with a prospect for a year is no big deal. Truth be told, following up until the end of time is no big deal because you have this system in place that puts order to the process.

You may start this prospecting timeline over numerous times before you get the business. Let's say on the one-month contact, the prospect actually answers the phone. She tells you she's sorry she hasn't gotten back to you, but she's been buried in a project that will be completed in two weeks. She asks you to follow up then. You'll document the conversation in the notes section and advance the reminder date two weeks. If you get her voicemail when you follow up in two weeks, you'll leave a message and then email or text, document in the notes section, and advance the reminder date for one week. You'll follow up in one week and if you get her voicemail, you'll leave a message, then send an email or text, document the notes section, and advance the reminder date for two weeks—so the timeline starts all over again. Every time you communicate with her, she'll tell you when the next follow-up date is because you'll always ask in the follow-up conversation. I want to repeat, this timeline is used only when a prospect isn't getting back to you.

It's important that you continue to stay in touch even if she's not responding, which is why you go to quarterly contacts. You don't want her to forget about you. If you know she had an interest in your product/service yet she isn't getting back to you, the only assumption you can make is there's something going on in her life that's preventing her from responding to you. Don't assume she's not interested because if you do that you're making the buying decision for her. May I respectfully say that you're not qualified to make that decision because you don't know what's going on in her life and you don't have a crystal ball.

Don't get discouraged. Stay in the game. There's future business waiting for you.

Depending on your sales cycle, you may need to adjust the prospecting timeline. What's important is you have the same timeline that will support effective follow up action and keep you in the game.

Be in the Elite 10%

When you implement the prospecting timeline and system, you'll be in the elite 10% and it's not hard at all to do because you have your CRM, your scheduled daily follow-up time and your systematized follow-up work schedule. Speaking in French terms, voilà, you're now in the elite 10%.

When you're documenting conversations, you don't have to write down every word verbatim. You just have to document enough to jog your memory, so when it comes time to make contact you'll recall the prior conversation. Some follow-up shorthand that can help you speed up the process when documenting is noted as follows:

SW—Spoke with
LM—Left message
EM—Email

VM—Voicemail
BD—Birthday
Thx—Thanks
Bs—Business
Mo—Month
Qt – Quote

FU—Follow-up
W/ - With
EM Response
— Use quotation marks
Rec'd—Received
CI—Checking In
JB—Just because
Wk—Week
Pres - Presentation
Prop - Proposal

An example of my notes would look like this using the shorthand:

3/12/15 – LM and EM'd. FU 3/19

3/19/15 – LM and EM'd. FU 4/2

4/2/15 – SW and she's interested, but is busy. Wants me to FU in 2 weeks. FU 4/16

4/16/15 – LM and EM'd. Rec'd EM "Thanks for your follow up Wanda. Still interested, but am going to need another couple of weeks. Check in with me then. Thank you!" FU 4/30

Can you see how simple it is to document actions and conversations? How much time do you think it would take to type those entries? Very little. Don't make something a bigger deal than it is. Stay out of your head and keep your resisting thoughts at bay.

As I did in the 4/16/15 entry, when you receive an email from a prospect, copy what's important in it and paste it into the notes section. Put quote marks at the beginning and end of what you pasted so you know where the email starts and ends. When the important information from an email is pasted in the notes section, you have immediate access to it, which prevents you from having to sift through a bunch of emails in your inbox, deleted items or other folders. Paste explanation points, smiley faces or whatever else the prospect has put in the email that expresses emotion. The explanation point in the illustration tells me that she's looking forward to me following up in two weeks. It's up to your own interpretation as to what you think is important.

Pasting important information from emails also reminds me to use the prospect's language. For example, I had a prospect I was working with regarding a workshop for his sales team. I emailed a proposal and followed up on it. He emailed me and said he submitted the "bid" to his Board. Now I would never refer to my proposal as a bid, but since that was his language, I referred to my proposal as a bid in my subsequent follow-up. This is a subtle way to deepen the connection with a prospect. It's called mirroring.

Chapter 8
Four Follow-up Musts

I've already mentioned that the customer service bar is low today and part of that poor service is the result of not being attentive to important relationships. I'm going to share four follow-up musts that when implemented and consistently practiced, will put you head and shoulders above your competition. These actions will also help deepen loyalty.

What is going to support your systems are timelines. I've already shared some timelines with you and you'll see that these four practices also have specific timelines. This is what will support consistent action and I'll say it again, consistency is what will change your business.

Follow-up Must #1

Nice to Meet You

The first follow-up must is taking care of new contacts within 24 hours or the next business day. We touched on this before. If you have a stack of business cards on your desk, that's an indicator that you more than likely haven't taken follow up action and you're not using a CRM. Because you take care of new contacts in Action #1 in your daily follow up work system, you will no longer have the issue of business card build up.

I mentioned earlier that research tells us 48% of people never follow up. I also said I believe this statistic is actually even higher and one of the reasons for my thinking is because of all the stacks of business cards I've seen on my customers' desks and the countless conversations I've had with others who have this same business card buildup problem.

Most likely the business cards sitting on your desk were collected from networking events or other business gatherings. What does this stack of business cards reflect?

- You go to an event, meet people, collect business cards and put them on your desk.
- A couple days go by and you haven't been able to follow up on those business cards because you've "been busy."
- Now it's been a couple weeks and you're feeling a little embarrassed and uncomfortable to follow up, so you do nothing.
- Now it's been a month and there's no way you're going to follow up because it's downright embarrassing and uncomfortable at this point.
- You go to another event, meet people, collect business cards and put them on your desk.
- The same cycle occurs over and over and before you know it, you have stacks of business cards sitting on your desk with which you've done nothing with.

Going to events takes time and money and time is money. Thus, if you're not doing anything to follow up with the people you meet, you're going to get the same result as if you never went. That's the bottom-line result of not taking action on new contacts.

Clear the Business Card Clutter

Business cards were not created to become décor on your desk or take up space in your drawers. The purpose of a business card is to transfer contact information from the card to your CRM and then you throw the card away.

If you have stacks of business cards on your desk, I want you go through them. There are going to be cards that belong to people you don't remember at all; you don't know where or when you met them and/or what conversation took place. I'm going to ask you to throw these cards away. I often get pushback when I suggest this, but if you're resistant to this idea, my challenging question to you is: *"why keep them"?* You don't know who these people are or where you met them, so what are the chances you're going to follow up? Slim to none and my bet is on none. Get rid of them; clear the clutter because I want you to have a clean slate.

This won't happen again because, as mentioned, in your daily follow-up work the first item you take care of is your new contacts. So, let the old cards go. This stale stack of cards is negative energy that's nothing more than a reminder of what you haven't done. You don't need that anymore.

For the business cards that are from people you do remember and wish you had followed up with, but didn't, you can easily bring that contact back to life by using the following scripting. It's a simple four-step process:

1. Remind her who you are, where you met and what the conversation was.

2. Admit you didn't follow up.

3. Apologize for not following up.

4. Move on to the purpose of your call.

Scripting

Hi Sally, this is Marie with ABC Marketing Company. We met at a chamber event a couple months ago and talked about your interest in creating some new marketing materials. I'm sorry I haven't followed up with you sooner. I thought I would follow up today to see if you're still interested. If so, is this a good time to talk?

The worst thing that will happen is she tells you she already had the work done with someone else. If so, chalk it up losing that business because you didn't follow up. However, remind yourself that it won't happen again because you now have your daily follow-up work system in place. What's important is you tried. If you didn't follow up, the answer would definitely be no. On the flip side of this scenario, it's possible she tells you she's still interested, but hasn't done anything because she's been too busy to think about it. The conversation will go from there. Remember, don't assume the prospect won't be interested because you didn't follow up when you should have. Let her tell you what the decision is.

Another way to organize your collection of business cards is to always have a pen with you when you're at an event. There are people who hand out their business cards like a poker dealer. They haven't spent any time with you and have no clue if you're interested in their business, but they give you their business card anyway. For these people, draw a diagonal line on their business card when they walk away. This way you'll know when you're doing your follow-up work the next day you can just throw that card away. You don't have to follow up with or keep the business card of every person you meet. I want you to only focus on the people with whom you have a connection. This way, you're not banging your head against a wall or wasting time on people who aren't interested in you or what you do.

When you meet people who you do have a connection with and/or are potential prospects or referral sources, jot down some notes on their business card after the conversation so when you get back to your office, you don't have to try and remember what was said. If you've met a lot of people, it can be difficult and stressful to recall names and conversations at a later time, even when it is the next day.

Follow-up Must #2

Do You Say Thank You?

Saying thank you is a common courtesy we were taught as children. My oh my, how that courtesy has gone by the wayside today for many adults. It's sad to say that the mere act of saying thank you will make you stand out and be different. As sad as that is, it's also great news for you because such a simple gesture is an easy way to wow those who are important to you.

I send gifts on a regular basis to primarily say thank you for a variety of reasons. I can tell you without exaggeration that 95% of the people I send gifts to never acknowledge them. This doesn't discourage me from sending them; it's merely an observation as to how much the simple act of saying thank you has gone out the window. To be honest, I'm always more surprised when someone does thank me for a gift than I am when they don't. I believe the reason people don't take time to acknowledge when someone has done something nice for them is they're in the immediate mindset thinking of, *"I don't have time, I'm too busy."* Stay out of that way of thinking. It will keep you from even the most common of courtesies.

An associate of mine gave me a great opportunity that was going to potentially have a big impact on my workshop business. As a thank you, I sent him a $100 American Express Gift Card. I never heard from him. I said earlier that I'm more surprised when someone does thank me than when they don't, but not hearing from this gentleman did surprise me. How often do you get a $100 gift card in the mail? I generally don't send gifts this large, but it was really important to me and I wanted to say thank you in a big way. After this experience, my lack of surprise when gifts aren't acknowledged went to a new level.

Thank You for Your Business

I want you to ask yourself out of everyone you do business with, who has thanked you? Think about your banker, insurance agent, financial planner, hairdresser, auto mechanic, dry cleaner, your favorite restaurant you frequent on a regular basis and others you do business with. I bet the majority of them haven't thanked you.

Now let me flip that question around: how many of your customers have you thanked?

Every one of your customers deserves a thank you. Regardless of how small a customer is, never forget to say thank you. Small customers can grow into big ones and they may also know people who could be large customers.

The timeline for your thank you for business should be within 24 hours. To systematize this, you'll want to know exactly what your thank you will be. Remember, systems prevent you from having to think, thereby saving you time.

Your thank you doesn't have to be elaborate. The reason is, regardless of what your thank you is, you're going to stand out. A simple thank you phone call goes a long way.

You can have one thank you for all your customers or you can use a scale based on the size of business that was transacted.

If you decide to send the same thank you to *all* customers, your system could be everyone gets a thank you card. If you decide to send a card, make sure you have a supply on hand so you don't have to run out and buy one every time you need to send one out. Also, have boilerplate thank you verbiage. This is still personalized because it's your heartfelt words, but by having boilerplate verbiage, you don't have to think about what to say each time. In general, you probably say the same thing to each customer you're thanking and that's why boilerplate verbiage works. This is how you systematize the task of saying thank you. Remember, systems put you in the flow of ease.

If you decide your thank you will be based on dollars transacted, you could use a scale as follows:

$1,000 and under: thank you call

$1,000 - $2,000: thank you card

$2,000 - $5,000: thank you card with a gift card

$5,000 - $10,000: thank you lunch

Again, the key to this system flowing is having the supplies in stock and creating boilerplate verbiage. If you have a team, make sure everyone is on board with the thank you system so you have consistency.

When I teach my workshops, I have the attendees write a thank you note to one of their customers. I don't tell them beforehand and don't hand out the thank you cards until it's time for the exercise. When I make the announcement, I have never had a workshop where an attendee or two or three don't freeze during that moment. I find this so interesting because saying thank you is such a simple gesture, but one that can catch someone so off guard that it turns him into a "deer in headlights." This exercise can shut down people to the point where they won't participate in the exercise. Saying thank you for some is so out of the ordinary and so uncomfortable, they would rather not do it. It always saddens me when this happens.

The art of communication is at great risk in the day and age we're living in. I was giving a presentation to a group of young adults, aged 18 to 22. I talked to them about making "just because calls" discussed in System 4. One of the audience members asked what to say when calling "just because." These kids are so used to the electronic tools they're losing the skill of verbal communication. I might add that I've been asked this question on more than one occasion from others who are older adults. Don't lose the beautiful art of communication.

Thank You For the Referral

As previously mentioned, referrals are the easiest leads you'll ever get. You have someone out there selling you and your products or services on your behalf. It's crucial that you take care of your referral sources. They are as important as your customers.

The timeline for your thank you for the referral should be within 24 hours.

Thanking referral sources is a two-step process:

1. Saying thank you when you get the referral.
2. Saying thank you if the referral turns into closed business.

Again, you'll want to decide what your thank you will be and have a stock of supplies on hand.

Thank You for the Opportunity

When someone gives you an opportunity, it's important to thank that person. The size of the opportunity will determine the type of thank you. Because these aren't as frequent as closed business or referrals, you won't have a system per se for this. The timeline for your thank you for the opportunity should be within 24 hours.

Thank You for Your Time

Time is valuable and it's something we'll never get back, so when someone gives you his time, it's important to thank him. This may be a prospect who agreed to meet with you, a customer who's looking for additional services, a referral source who agreed to hear about a new product you're offering or someone who volunteered her time for a cause for you. There may be many other reasons someone has given you their time and a thank you is appropriate for all of them. Again, these aren't as frequent as the other thank yous, so you won't have a system per se for this. The timeline for your thank you for your time should be within 24 hours.

You don't have to worry about finding time to get your thank yous out because you'll do this work during your daily follow-up time. You have time allocated for admin work in your daily follow up work system. Because you have daily follow-up time, getting this work done is part of your day, *not* an addition to it. Therefore, getting your thank yous out is a "no brainer."

Follow-up Must #3
What Do You Do After 30 Days?

I talked earlier about doing business with someone and never hearing from that person again. This is not a good feeling if you're the customer and it's not a good practice if you're the businessperson.

In the *Follow Up Sales Strategies System*, you will always make a 30-day check-in call. When business is closed, you'll go into your CRM and set up a reminder date for 30 days to make this call. This will be very easy to do because in your daily follow-up work, Action #2, you take care of reminders for the current day. The purpose of this phone call is to see how the customer is doing with the purchased product/service and if he has any other needs. You can also thank him again for his business. This is such a powerful way to show you haven't forgotten about him. This is the type of attention builds loyalty.

Follow-up Must #4
Happy Birthday To You...Happy Birthday To You

This is the easiest way to show someone you're thinking about him—when it has nothing to do with your business. With the *Follow Up Sales Strategies System*, you'll send a birthday card and then make a birthday phone call. When sending the birthday card, don't include your business card. Wonder why not? The reason is because the purpose of the card is about his birthday, not your business. You may also be thinking *"what's the big deal, I can kill two birds with one stone."* Let me remind you that this is immediate mindset thinking. What you'd be doing is turning the birthday contact into a multi-purpose contact. Multi-tasking is not all it's cracked up to be and it's highly overrated. When you create multi-purpose contacts, you're diluting each purpose. Wouldn't it have a much more meaningful impact if the purpose of your contact is solely about his birthday and nothing to do with your business? Don't come across as having a hidden agenda. I know that sounds strong, but isn't it true? When you include your business card it looks like you're using his birthday as an opportunity to remind him about what you do. This is not a good practice.

What if the recipient won't know who you are without your business card enclosed? That's simple: you shouldn't be sending a birthday card until you've invested enough in the relationship that he knows who you are without your business card. Birthdays are personal, so don't be afraid to take the necessary time to develop the relationship before you implement the birthday system.

A question I'm asked frequently is how to ask for someone's birthday. It's very simple and you don't make it a big deal. You say, *"I have your contact information and would like to include your birthday. If you're OK with that, I just need the month and day."* Some people are sensitive about their age, so this can put them at ease by not having to provide the year they were born. You'll find the majority of the time, people are more than happy to give their birthday information. Once in a while someone will say he doesn't celebrate birthdays. If so, ask a follow up question: *"Do you celebrate holidays?"* If the answer is *no*, it's most likely for religious reasons. Make a note of that in your notes section and reach out in ways that don't include birthday and holidays. If you're not comfortable asking for someone's birthday, that's an indicator that you haven't invested enough time. Keep investing.

Birthday calls are so powerful. They're my favorite time of day. If you get the birthday person on the phone, it's so nice to catch up. You'll find out how he's doing and what's going on in his life. This call has nothing to do with business. Now, having said that, I could do a whole workshop on the business I've gotten from birthday calls. I want to be very clear that my intention for the birthday call is NEVER to get business. In fact, I don't ever bring up my business. But what ends up happening is the birthday boy wants to know how I'm doing and how my business is going, and before I know it I'm hanging up with a referral or more business without asking for it. The reason this happens is because human nature kicks in. When you consistently show someone you care about him and remember him, he'll want to help you even when you haven't asked for it. This help can come in many forms, including more business, referrals, time and opportunity.

I don't want you to think about starting to make birthday calls so you can get more business. This won't work, because you're coming from the wrong place and it won't be genuine. You can always tell when someone is being phony or has a hidden agenda.

I have an associate who booked me for a speaking engagement a couple of years ago for his business association. I haven't seen him since I spoke at his event, but I've stayed in touch with him. I called him recently for his birthday and as so often happens, he asked me how I was doing and asked about my business. He then told me he had two events coming up in the next month and said he would be interested in booking me. He said he would get back to me to let me know if he could get me on the agenda. It's like he was doing me a favor all because I gave him a birthday call. He called me back a few days later and I was booked. This happens time and time again for me. I believe it's the old adage at work: "what you send out comes back." I'll add another word to this adage: "what you *genuinely* send out comes back."

Birthday cards and calls leave an outstanding impression. There's no replacement for them. You can wish someone well on her birthday through electronic means such as an Ecard, Facebook, LinkedIn or any other electronic tool, but that doesn't take much effort or thought and being that this is how the masses send birthday wishes today, there's nothing special about it. Doing so electronically is better than doing nothing at all, but it's not nearly as impressionable. If you're going to send a birthday wish, make it count, wow the birthday person, stand out and be different. Sending a card and making a phone call is going to take very little time—time that you have allocated in your daily follow-up work. You'll get the birthday card out in Action #3 and you'll make the birthday call in Action #2. This is an important way that you'll take care of your relationships and build loyalty.

I was speaking at an event and afterward a woman came up to me. Her birthday was the day before and she told me she got 25 birthday wishes. I found it interesting that she counted them. She continued to tell me that of the 25 wishes, one was a call, two were cards she received in the mail and the other 22 were electronic wishes. She proceeded to tell me that the 22 electronic wishes did mean a lot to her. She obviously felt I was knocking electronic wishes, which was not my intent. I asked her of the 25 birthday wishes she received, which were most memorable. She said the birthday phone call was the most memorable. I then asked what the next most memorable wish was and she said the two birthday cards. That was my point. Cards and calls are far more memorable than electronic wishes. Had I asked her to name the 22 people who wished her well electronically, I bet she wouldn't have been able to remember all of them. My question to you is, do you want to be in the top three or the 22?

Another comment I often hear is, *"I'm not a birthday person."* My response is *you* may not be, but your customers, prospects and referral sources may be. If it's a matter of just being uncomfortable sending birthday wishes, then do it. Remember, you can't grow in your comfort zone, so bust out of it. If birthdays just truly do not resonate with you, then don't do it. Reach out in other ways.

Chapter 9
Secure Your Top 20%

How important are the top 20% of your clientele, prospects and referral sources? I hope your answer is VERY. If they're important to you, how well are you taking care of them? The best way to take care of and secure your top 20% is through following up and staying in touch. This is what's going to create loyalty and loyalty is how security is built. I'll say it again, what lies at the heart of loyalty is appreciation. Do you see how one is the result of another?

Appreciation = Loyalty = Security

Who Are Your Top 20%?

When I ask this question, it is not uncommon for me to hear "I'm not really sure." This obviously is not a good answer. When I hear this, it tells me there's not much attention being paid to the top relationships that are so important.

You must know who your top 20% are. Here are some ways you can define them:

Prospects

Size of potential business

How close you are to getting the business

Other opportunities that will come from converting the prospect to a customer

Customers

Dollar size of business that has been transacted

Number of transactions they've done with you

Length of time they've been a customer

Referral Sources

Number of referrals they've given

Number of the referrals that have turned into closed business

They understand your business, which results in not wasting your time on bad referrals

Once you've defined your top 20%, it's time to identify who they are. Completing the following worksheet will help you do that. Start by writing down your top five customers, prospects and referral sources in the Name column. In the second column, Date, write down the last time you had verbal communication with them. In the third column, Where/Who, write down how you met the person. Was it a referral, a cold call, at a networking event or some other way? In the last column, Date, write down the last time you talked to the person who referred you and/or the last time you attended the event where you met the person. I want you to have total awareness as to how attentive you're being to these very important people.

TOP 5 PROSPECTS

	Name	Date	Where / Who	Date
1)				
2)				
3)				
4)				
5)				

TOP 5 CUSTOMERS

	Name	Date	Where / Who	Date
1)				
2)				
3)				
4)				
5)				

TOP 5 REFERRAL SOURCES

	Name	Date	Where / Who	Date
1)				
2)				
3)				
4)				
5)				

Once the list is completed, ask yourself if your competition would like to have it. Of course they would. There's only one way to protect yourself from your competition accessing these very important people and that is to take care of them.

This exercise may make you squirm if you realize you haven't been attentive. My intention is not to make you feel bad; it's to make you aware. Once you're aware of how you're handling your relationships, that's when the door opens for change.

This exercise will give you an immediate action plan on the relationships you need to start taking care of, investing in and showing appreciation to so you can start building loyalty. Once you've contacted everyone on this list, go to your next top five customers, prospects and referral sources. Keep going until you've reached your top 20%

I was teaching a workshop and had the attendees complete this exercise. Afterward, a woman came up to me literally in tears. She said couldn't come up with five customers and realized she was in denial about her business. This was a real eye opener for her.

If you find yourself in the same situation, I've provided some suggestions to build your list of customers, prospects and referral sources.

To build your prospect list/pipeline:

- Look at the business cards on your desk and make contact with the people you didn't follow up with and wished you had as discussed in Chapter 8.
- Attend networking events.

- Ask for referrals.
- Make cold calls.

To build your customer list:

- Follow up with *all* your prospects.
- Think about the top customers you had at another company or when you were in another industry. While they may not be current customers, you can rekindle those relationships and see if there's an opportunity to get these people as customers where you are now or maybe they know someone who'd be interested in your product/service.
- Determine if your existing customers are in need of additional products/services.

To build your referral source list:

- Attend networking events.
- Ask for referrals.
- Cold call.

Most people aren't crazy about cold calling or they're afraid to do it. However, it's always an option. It's better than sitting around twiddling your thumbs and staring at a thin pipeline. Taking action is the only way to build your pipeline—and having a robust pipeline is critical to securing new customers.

What About Cold Calling?

I cold call on a regular basis for my corporate workshops. It's become a challenge for me that I actually get a kick out of. Call me crazy. I know getting warm leads and referrals are more effective and less time-consuming ways to build your business than cold calling. I'm certainly always on the lookout for warm leads and referrals, but I still use cold calling as one my business-building practices.

I cold called a well-known company in San Diego. I sent a cover letter and flyer outlining the details of my workshop to the President. When I was doing my research on the company, I couldn't find the person in charge of sales, so I went to the top. I made two follow-up contacts, to no apparent avail. I then decided to contact the Human Resources Director, since oftentimes, Human Resources is involved with training decisions. I made three follow-up contacts and still no response. One day I was leaving a meeting and had just gotten into my car when my phone rang. The person calling me was in charge of sales at this company. He said he'd received my information from both the President and the Human Resources Director and wanted to talk to me about teaching my workshop at one of their sales meetings. It appeared nothing was happening with the information I sent to the President and Human Resources Director, but if I'd assumed they weren't interested and stopped following up, I'm sure that call never would have been made. I got the business and taught my workshop to their broker team.

"We appreciated Wanda Allen sharing her ***Follow Up Workshop****. I believe it will provide our brokers with excellent client/prospect follow up tools to implement as well as reinforcing current follow up practices. I personally saw opportunities to enhance my own follow up activities and touch contacts with clients."*

— Marc Doyle, SIOR, CCIM, Director
Cassidy Turley San Diego

I continue to stay in touch with Marc and was able to refer him one of my clients who was looking to sell his building. Marc transacted business with my client. This is the power of follow-up at work. Not only did my cold-calling efforts get me business, but I also was able to return the favor to Marc by giving him business. It's a beautiful process!

Are You Paying Attention to Your Top 20%?

Once you've defined your top 20% and know who they are, it's time to start paying attention to them. The only way you can do this is to follow up and stay in touch on a consistent basis. You will use your CRM to help you track your efforts. I'm going to suggest you stay in touch four times a year, which is once a quarter. If you're thinking that's a lot, I'm going to say it's not when you take into consideration that this is your top 20% we're talking about. If you don't take care of them, someone else will. If you don't feel four times a year is enough and want to stay in touch more frequently, just be sure it's manageable so you can be consistent.

Your top 20% are your crème de la crème.
Take good care of them.

Does Your Top 20% Feel Appreciated?

It's crucial that your top 20% knows how much you appreciate them. In the fast-paced world we live in, it can be easy to forget about the importance of showing appreciation. The best and only way to do this is to pay attention to the relationship. When you consistently stay in touch, you will consistently pay attention to your relationships. How you do this is detailed later in System #4.

It can be of great value to collect personal information on your customers, prospects and referral sources, such as their favorite restaurant for breakfast, lunch and dinner, their favorite wine, if they drink coffee, their hobbies, if they like sporting events, and whatever else you'd like to know about them. You can gather this information by simply asking for it or you can listen closely during your conversations to see if they reveal some of their personal "likes." Keep this information in the notes section of your CRM. It comes in handy when you want to appreciate someone in a unique way; your personalization efforts will make them feel very special.

To gauge how much appreciation you're showing or the level of appreciation those in your top 20% are feeling, ask yourself the following questions:

- Do I make her feel important?
- Am I excited when I talk to him?
- Am I grateful for her business/relationship?
- Am I attentive to his needs when I talk to him?
- Have I done anything special for her lately or ever?

If you can answer yes to all these questions, I guarantee you're showing an appropriate amount of appreciation and your customers, prospects, and referral sources are feeling properly appreciated.

Don't lose the excitement and appreciation for your customers, current and past. You should always hold them in the same regard you did when they were new. They deserve this. The last thing you want to do is take them for granted.

Are Your Top 20% Vulnerable Prey?

The only way to keep your competitors from trying to nosh on your customer base, referral sources and prospecting pipeline is to be sure you have loyalty. If you're not sure how loyal your people are, you need to start investing immediately. You will have a much greater peace of mind knowing that your top 20% and beyond aren't vulnerable prey.

System #4

Consistently Staying in Touch

As has been mentioned, you'll stay in touch with your top 20% on a quarterly basis.

For those who **aren't** in your top 20%, decide how often you want to stay in touch. I suggest no less than three times a year.

To determine who you'll put in your staying-in-touch system, ask yourself the following questions:

- Do I like this person?
- Do I have a connection with this person?
- Do I want a relationship with this person?

Keep the focus on the relationship. It's hard to genuinely stay in touch with someone you really don't like or aren't that interested in. Don't make efforts to stay in touch if you're only doing it to *get* something; you'll come across as insincere and self-serving. Being authentic is a must.

As I mentioned earlier, you want all your contacts to be single purpose. When you have just one purpose, your contacts will be more meaningful, you'll express a deeper level of appreciation and the effort will be far more powerful.

> I did business with an associate of mine. After the sale was closed, I received a card from her. She thanked me for my business, suggested other products I should try, asked for a referral and wished me a Happy 4th of July...all in one card.

Talk about a multi-purpose contact. This was way too much. She diluted each purpose. Had she sent me a card for any one of those purposes, it would have been far more impactful. The card was so full it didn't really impress me in the way I'm sure she intended it to. This is why multi-purpose contacts aren't effective.

> When I released my first book, I received a congratulations card from an associate. After she congratulated me, she then went on to tell me about her upcoming seminar.

I couldn't help but wonder whether she really wanted to congratulate me or use my book release as an opportunity to promote her seminar. While she may have had the good intention of congratulating me, it was completely discounted by the promotion of her seminar. Had she just congratulated me with no self-promotion, it would have been far more meaningful.

I hope these examples help you understand why single-purpose contact is so much better.

Plan your three to four touches a year around an important date, such as the person's birthday, the anniversary of business or the date you met him.

If you're staying in touch four times a year, your quarterly touches will start from the important date and go out quarterly from there so you're always coming back around on the important date. For example, if the important date you choose is the person's birthday, which is January 11, you'll touch her on that day. The other three touches will be on April 11, July 11, October 11 and back again on January 11. This also creates balance so you're not touching everyone at the same time. If you interact with someone in between your designated months to make contact, don't change the schedule; just chalk it up to touching that person more than four times that year.

If you're staying in touch three times a year, your touches will start from the important date and go from there. If the important date you choose is anniversary of business, which is October 23, you'll touch him on that day, then the other contacts will be February 23, June 23 and back again on October 23. Again, if you interact with someone in between your designated months to make contact, don't change the schedule; just chalk it up to touching that person more than three times that year.

What kind of touches you make will vary. With the *Follow Up Sales Strategies System*, you'll alternate touches. One touch will be about your business and the next touch will be about something that has nothing to do with your business. This creates a very nice balance and supports you in investing in the relationship beyond business.

Another benefit of staying in touch is it affords you the opportunity to remind the person you're touching about you and your business. She needs to be reminded. Don't assume she'll remember. If you're not staying in touch and keeping her updated on your business, she's likely to forget. It's your responsibility to make sure people remember who you are and what you do. When you're not remembered, you'll lose business. That's why consistently staying in touch is paramount as a business-building tool.

My parents have a neighbor named Steve who owns a flooring company. Steve has been my parents' neighbor for years. They see each other often in a neighborly way, waving hi when pulling in or out of the garage and yelling, "how are you" from across the street. When my parents remodeled their living room and kitchen, Steve saw the work trucks and curiosity brought him over to see what they were doing. My dad told him they were remodeling and were going to use his flooring services when they got to that point. Steve told him he had his general contractor's license and could have overseen the entire remodel. The problem was, my dad didn't know that. He thought Steve just did flooring. Because Steve didn't keep my parents updated on his business, he had to watch his competition work on his neighbor's house.

I had a prospect who owns a car dealership. He was trying to determine if he needed my services. He believed since he sold cars, his customers wouldn't forget about him because a car is one of the biggest purchases a person makes. I told him that's not true and I know this from personal experience. When I purchased my condo, the Realtor I used was great. She was professional, friendly and handled the transaction with no problems. I never heard from her again after escrow closed. I can't remember her name or the company she worked for. All I remember is she had blonde hair. I wouldn't know her if she were standing in front of me. I told my prospect that a home purchase is bigger than a car purchase and going by his philosophy, I should not have forgotten about my Realtor, but I have because I've never heard from her. It's your responsibility to make sure you're not forgotten about.

One of the touches should include at least one phone call or in-person meeting per year in particular for your top 20%. Verbal communication is very important and can't be replaced by any other tool in the box. As discussed earlier, use all the tools in your toolbox to keep it interesting and mixed up.

You'll always document every touch you make in your notes section so you can keep track of what you've done.

All it takes to stay on top of these touches is using your reminder dates and notes section. You'll get this all-important work done during your follow-up time, in Action #2, when you take care of current reminders for the day.

When you're consistently staying in touch, you're guaranteed to have better relationships, more loyalty, and the opportunity for more business and referrals.

Following are some ideas for staying in touch. Get creative and be different.

Business-Building (Money-Making) Touches

- Ask for a referral.
- Follow up for a meeting.
- Follow up for next step.
- Follow up on a decision to do business with you.
- Make a cold call.

Relationship-Building Touches

- Ask for birthday information.
- Bring lunch in for the staff.
- Celebrate the anniversary of business.

- Check in to see how the customer is doing with your product/service.
- Email an industry tip that's not in newsletter format.
- Go to a sporting event/give tickets to a sporting event.
- Hold a Lunch-n-Learn at the customer's office.
- Make a "just because" call to see how the customer is doing. This call is NOT about business.
- Make a LinkedIn recommendation.
- Play golf / tennis.
- Request a LinkedIn or Facebook connection.
- Set up a meeting for coffee, lunch, dinner or drinks.
- Send a birthday wish.
- Send a card.
- Send a holiday wish/gift.
- Send a promotional product.
- Send something of interest or value to the customer that's not about your business.
- Send a thank you for business call, card or gift.
- Send a thank you for referral call, card or gift.
- Share a testimonial you recently received.
- Stop by the office to say hi.

Miscellaneous Touches

- Ask for a testimonial.
- Send an eNewsletter.
- Send an email with a video or podcast link that would be of interest.

The touches are self-explanatory, but I do I want to highlight a few of them:

Celebrate the Anniversary of Business

This is a really great touch. When you're tracking a customer's anniversary of doing business with you, it shows you're really paying attention to the relationship. If you operate a transactional business, you can still track anniversaries. This is most impressive, because you're not seeing the customer on a regular basis through repeat business.

Create traditions around the anniversary. If you work for an employer, take the customer to lunch with the President/owner, Sales Manager or anyone else who plays a significant role in the company. You might bring in lunch for your customer's staff, or your tradition might be something as simple as a phone call or meeting for coffee.

Ask For a Referral

Please get in this habit. This is a great way to build your pipeline and increase your business. As I said earlier, when you effectively invest in your relationships, it will be very comfortable to ask for referrals. A payoff of investing well is you get to do business with people your customers know. This is powerful; don't forget to do it.

Ask For a Testimonial

When you have transacted business and the customer is satisfied, you would be remiss not to ask for a testimonial. I know a lot of people are uncomfortable asking for one. If this is you, you have to get out of your comfort zone and start asking. Testimonials are great prospecting tools that can help you land future business.

If you know you have a satisfied customer, once business

has been transacted, you would simply ask, *"if you feel like my services/products have helped you, would you be open to writing a testimonial?"* That's it…nothing uncomfortable about it at all. You'll also tell him that you'll send an email reminding him about the testimonial request and give him a couple of ideas on what he can talk about. Make it as easy on him as you can. The easier it is, the more likely he'll do it. I read an article that said only 40% of people who say they'll give a testimonial will actually do it. So if you don't get one, don't take it personally; just remember this statistic. The only thing you have control over is your action. Ask for the testimonial and rest easy knowing you've done your part.

Here's how my testimonial email request is written:

Hi Chad,

I'm always looking to add to my book of testimonials and would like to ask for a favor. If your team has experienced improvements in their sales performance and/or relationships as a result of the systems and timelines I taught in my workshop, would you be open to writing a testimonial? A couple of ideas to talk about are what problem my workshop helped your team solve or what improvements they experienced as a result of the workshop. A sentence or two would be great.

I'm giving him ideas on what to talk about and telling him that a sentence or two will suffice. Easy, peasy; it works very well.

If you have past customers from whom you would like to request a testimonial, that's easy to do as well, as noted in the following.

Scripting

Hi Joe,

I've decided to build a book of testimonials for my business. I'm reaching out to see if you'd be open to writing a testimonial for the service we provided for your company. A couple of ideas to talk about are what problem our service helped your company solve or what improvements you've experienced as a result of our service. A sentence or two would be great."

Another way to get a testimonial is when you receive a thank you message from a customer. There's *always* a testimonial inside a thank you, although you may need to reword it to get it in testimonial format. Always ask for permission to use it as a testimonial and if you've reworded it, send an email with the testimonial format to request his approval of the changes.

I have a business associate who runs a networking group comprised primarily of sales professionals. I spoke at one of his events and afterward I received a thank you card in the mail. I sent him an email requesting his permission to use his thank you as a testimonial. The email read as follows:

(the subject line was: Favor)

Hi Ken,

I received your thank you card. I really appreciate your kind words. In reading your thank you, I see a testimonial in there. My favor is would you be OK if I used your words as a testimonial?

It would read as follows:

Wanda, thank you so very much for your wonderful presentation! Every time I talk to you and hear you speak, I come away with new tips and lots of reminders about how to

> *build and maintain relationships.*
>
> **Ken Schmitt**
>
> President,
> Turning Point Executive Search and the Sales Leadership Alliance

I received this email back:

> *Wanda, I would be happy to provide that testimonial.*

Don't pass up opportunities for testimonials and don't be afraid to ask.

When you get a testimonial, keep it in your "Book of Testimonials," which is a Word document where you'll house them all. When you're prospecting, especially cold calling, always include testimonials. Match like industries, if possible. That's why it's great to have testimonials from a variety of companies and industries.

> I was speaking at an event and a catering manager from a well-known prestigious golf club was in the audience. She came up to me after the event and said she would love to get me into the club to teach one of my workshops to their team. She wasn't the decision-maker and needed to talk to the General Manager. I told her I would send her a proposal along with details on the workshop for her manager. I also included a few testimonials. Her manager doesn't know me "from Adam," so it's always good to include third-party reviews. My proposal was accepted and we booked a date for the workshop. The General Manager told me he wasn't going to be able to attend, but he came in for a few minutes in the beginning to introduce me. During the introduction, he said he knew one of the people who had given me a testimonial that I included in my proposal package. The

testimonials I submitted weren't from anyone in his industry because I didn't have any, so I included a few of my best ones. He told his team during the introduction that he called the person who gave me the testimonial and got good feedback. I know this definitely played a part in his decision to bring me in. This is the power of testimonials. Don't let a satisfied customer go without asking for a testimonial.

"A BIG thank you for sharing your ***Follow Up Sales Strategies*** *workshop and wealth of knowledge with our sales team. We all have lofty goals and you really gave us some valuable insights on how we can get there with a simple, straightforward plan of action! I'm very excited to implement the ideas".*

— Katy Arrington, Senior Catering Sales Manager
Maderas Golf Club

The General Manager mentioned that he had some associates who have sales teams that might be interested in my workshop and he would be happy to pass on their contact information. He had to leave so I didn't get them that day. I taught the workshop just before the holidays and decided to wait until after the 1st of the year to ask for the referrals. When I contacted him, he gave me eight referrals. All I had to do was follow up and ask for them. As of this writing, I've received two noes, 1 person is passing on my information to the decision- maker and I'm waiting to hear from the other five. Do you see how you can build your business from the people you already know? It works!

Send Holiday Wishes/Gifts

Holidays are a great way to touch your contacts. With the *Follow Up Sales Strategies System*, you'll think outside the December holiday "box." The problem with sending holiday cards in December is so many others do it. It's not unique or different and there's nothing special about it. If you do send cards out in December, get them out no later than the first week of the month. If they go any out later than that, you'll get caught in with the masses. For all you know, a receptionist or administrative assistant is opening your card and taping it to the wall without the intended recipient ever seeing it or knowing you've reached out.

If your card goes out early in the month, you'll stand out. You'll be thought of as being organized and ahead of schedule, which will leave a great impression. You may also choose to stand out by sending cards for Thanksgiving or New Year's instead of the traditional December holiday greetings. Not many send cards for these occasions.

There are many other holidays throughout the year. If you Google holidays in any given year, most months have between two and four. Think about reaching out on Valentine's Day, St. Patrick's Day, Cinco de Mayo, 4th of July, Halloween, etc. There are many ways to be different during holiday times.

Remember the purpose for staying in touch is multi-faceted:

- You're investing in the relationship to show appreciation.
- You're investing in the relationship to create loyalty.
- You're reminding them about you and your business.
- You're able to comfortably ask for something if you're in need, i.e., referrals, more business, etc.

I made a just because call to one of my clients. Her assistant told me she was out on medical leave. My client had a brain tumor. I was shocked. Thankfully it was benign. I called her at home and was able to express my well wishes to her. Had I not had her in my staying-in-touch system and didn't know about her health problem, I would have felt terrible if I had learned about it at a much later date or heard about it "through the grapevine". Because of my attentiveness to the relationship, I found out simply by staying in touch. I was so grateful for my system.

A goal you can set for yourself is to make one relationship-building touch and one money-making touch every day. The following calculation demonstrates the result of committing to this:

1 money-making touch per day + 1 relationship-building touch per day = 2

2 x 5 working days per week = 10

10 x 4 weeks per month = 40 touches per month

If you made 40 touches a month for one year, imagine what impact that would have on your business. Just two touches a day could turn into incredible results.

If you're going to set this as a goal, determine who your touches will be the night before so you don't have to spend time the next day trying to figure that out. Preparation is a big component of success. You can get these touches done during your follow-up time.

Chapter 10
Don't Leave Business on the Table

I'm sure at this point, you understand how not following up and staying in touch can adversely affect your success. When you're prospecting, if you're not staying in the game and making as many contacts as necessary to convert your prospect to a customer, you're going to leave that business on the table for someone else to get.

If you're not staying in touch with your customers beyond business reasons, you're going to jeopardize loyalty and be at risk of losing potential future business, potential referrals or the complete loss of the relationship.

If You Don't Follow Up, Someone Else Will

I want you to take this to heart. If you don't take care of your relationships, there's always someone out there who will. It's just a matter of time. Don't justify not being attentive with the following thoughts:

"He's fine."

"I'm too busy."

"He wouldn't leave."

"She knows I'm here."

"She's happy with our product/service."

"If he needs something, he'll let me know."

This is very dangerous thinking. These are thoughts that are characteristic of taking your relationships for granted. They're nothing more than assumptions. You don't know how people are unless you're communicating with them. Don't fool yourself.

Do You Know What Happens When You Assume?

Assuming is never, ever a good practice. Filling your head with assumptive thoughts is going to result in lost business and lost relationships.

Assuming is nothing more than making up a story to fit the situation you're in. You have to use your imagination when you assume. It's not logical. It's based on your opinion and past experiences, and oftentimes it will prevent you from taking action.

What happens when you assume?

You make an ASS out of U and ME = ASSUME

It doesn't serve anyone well. Don't do it!

Chapter 11
Outshine Your Competition

Customer service is not what it used to be. What's worse is we've become accustomed to experiencing par level service as OK. When I started my banking career in 1984, customer service was drilled into our heads. We had training after training on the subject. We had inside trainers and outside trainers. One bank I worked for actually hired "shoppers" who would come in and pretend they were customers—when what they were really doing was rating our service. They would complete a report and send it to the bank President. You talk about being kept on your toes. This all happened early in my career. Then I'd say for the last 10-15 years of my career, customer service training all but disappeared. I'm not sure where along the line the importance of customer service was lost. Mediocre service runs rampant today and has become the norm. Whenever I have an exceptional customer service experience I always take note and think, *"wow, they must have a great training program."* Sadly, I don't think that very often.

If you fully implement the *Follow Up Sales Strategies System*, I promise you your customer service skills will strengthen tremendously.

Make Your Customers, Prospects and Referral Sources Feel Important

With the *Follow Up Sales Strategies System* implemented, you'll never have to worry about your customers, prospects and referral sources not feeling important. It will absolutely happen because of the attention you'll be giving them through the practice of consistently staying in touch and showing appreciation. Everyone wants to feel important. We want to know we're important to those with whom we do business. Keep your systems in place and there will never be any doubt.

Why Do Customers Leave?

There was a study done that showed the following:

82% of customers left a company because of customer service.

Source: The Customer Experience Impact 2010 Report

This shows that customers usually don't leave because of issues with pricing, convenience or location…but disappointing customer service. That figure—82%—is really high. Since it takes more time, energy and money to get new customers than it does to keep the ones you have, strengthening your customer service skills, will increase your customer retention. With your staying-in-touch systems in place, you'll consistently display excellent customer service skills.

A great definition of customer service is, find out what your customers want and make sure they get it. I love this definition. It puts into perspective how important the customer is and that your primary business purpose is to ensure your customers are well taken care of. They're the lifelines to business.

If you've had a great customer service experience, I'm sure you'd agree it made you feel good, you remembered the experience, you want to continue to do business with the person who treated you so well, and you're open to referring that person/business. When you follow up and stay in touch, you're giving exceptional service. Your customers will remember you, they'll feel good about you, they'll want to continue to do business with you and they'll tell others about you.

Traits of exceptional service include:

- You return phone calls and emails in a timely manner.
- You're **ALWAYS** friendly.
- You don't appear rushed or hurried.
- You make your customers, prospects and referral sources feel important.
- You show appreciation.

If you display these traits, you'll be seen as being attentive and respectful of your relationships. If you don't exhibit them, you run the risk of becoming neglectful of your relationships. Don't run around in a frenzied state of mind and forget about the importance of serving and taking care of your customers in an exceptional way. Don't be impatient with your customers, prospects and referral sources. View them as VIPs. Have a "roll out the red carpet" mentality every time you deal with them. Let them know you're excited about working with them and you appreciate them. Be conscious of your energy level. Be willing to always go the extra mile.

Here's a good reality check: think about how big your customer fan club would be. Would the people you work with willingly be in your fan club? If not, there's only one fix: improve your customer service skills. Do this and you will establish the reputation of a quality person with whom to do business. The most important distinction between you and your competition is your level of service.

Seven Questions When Answered Yes Will Guarantee Exceptional Customer Service

1. Is my customer, prospect or referral source happy?

You know when someone is happy. You can hear it in their voice. If you don't feel satisfaction from a customer, prospect or referral source, you need to rethink how you handled the contact from start to finish. Think about every person you do business with being a potential member of your fan club. When you have a big fan club, you have a lot of great relationships and the potential for a lot of success. It's much easier to keep them happy than it is to try replacing them. Always provide a quality experience.

2. Is my boss happy or if I had a boss would she be happy?

If you work for someone, it's important that person is happy with you. There's a great peace of mind that comes along with that. Knowing your boss trusts your business practices and is aware that you always provide exceptional service is a great confidence booster.

If you are the boss, ask yourself whether a hypothetical boss would be happy with you. Not having anyone to report to can leave room for slack. If you're the boss, don't lose sight of the importance of providing exceptional customer service.

3. Will customers come back if they need further products/services?

You know that 82% of customers leave because of customer service. Thus, if your service isn't good, chances are customers won't come back. It doesn't take much to provide exceptional service: being attentive, responding in a timely manner and showing customers they're important to you. That's it.

4. Will customers refer me?

You have to be good if you want to be referable. You want everyone you're working with to have confidence in how you handle business and your relationships. This is what makes you referable.

5. Did I do the best job I could have?

When you haven't done your best, there are four primary reasons:

1. You were in a hurry.
2. You didn't take time to fully understand the needs of the person you're working with.
3. You lost sight of your appreciation for the person you're working with.
4. You weren't focused on providing exceptional service.

If you will focus on these four areas, you will absolutely do the best job possible every time. It's uncomfortable if you're the customer and you're having to deal with someone who is displaying any of these four traits.

6. Did I represent my company well?

It's vitally important to always be a great representative of the company you work for and that includes your own company, if you're self-employed. You do this by walking the talk, keeping your promises and staying professional at all times. When you look good and do well, your company looks good and does well.

7. If I were in my customers' shoes, would I be happy with the level of service I gave?

This is a very easy way to measure how you did. Don't justify why you would be happy even though *this* happened or *that* happened. Bottom line, all things considered, would you be happy with the service you provided? Would you be happy with the professional habits you displayed such as response time and quality of work? This is a great self-assessment thought process. Be honest.

Conclusion

As you begin putting the *Follow Up Sales Strategies System* in place, you may question yourself and the systems. That's your ego fighting against change. The ego doesn't like change and it doesn't like to be uncomfortable. But, remember, there's no room for growth in your comfort zone. If at any time you're getting uncomfortable, that's your signal to keep moving, keep pressing forward, and stay committed to these systems and timelines.

Many times, when you're thinking and operating from an ego standpoint, you can enter an irrational state of mind. You can talk yourself into or out of anything. Be very careful not to talk yourself out of implementing this system because it's uncomfortable. Again, this system is nothing more than a habit. As with any new behavior you want to turn into a habit, it's uncomfortable when you start. Once the habit is formed, it will be uncomfortable not to do it. Before you know it, working in the *Follow Up Sales Strategies System* will become second nature.

The following poem can help put your comfort zone into perspective:

I used to have a Comfort Zone
Where I knew I couldn't fail

The same four walls of busy work
Were really more like jail

I longed so much to do the things
I'd never done before
But stayed inside my Comfort Zone
And paced the same old floor

I claimed to be so busy
With the things inside my Zone
But deep inside I longed for
Something special of my own

I couldn't let my life go by
Just watching others win
I held my breath and stepped outside
To let the change begin

I took a step and with new strength
I'd never felt before
I kissed my Comfort Zone "goodbye"
And closed and locked the door

If you are in a Comfort Zone
Afraid to venture out
Remember that all winners were
At one time filled with doubt

A step or two and words of praise
Can make your dreams come true

Greet your future with a smile
Success is there for you

— Author Unknown

One thing I know to be true is that successful people take consistent action, have strong relationships and have excellent habits. You can achieve that with the teachings in this book. I want you to become a high-level performer. To do that, you have to consciously commit to performing at your highest level every day, even when you're uncomfortable.

I've given you a lot of information and your head is probably swimming with thoughts, ideas and excitement about implementing your follow-up systems. I want to recap the most critical parts of the *Follow Up Sales Strategies System*:

- Schedule your daily follow-up time (System 1)
- Systematize your daily follow-up work (System 2)
    1. Take care of new contacts
    2. Take care of the current daily reminders
    3. Take care of your admin follow-up work
- Always have the follow-up conversation (scripting in Chapter 7)
- Use the prospecting timeline (System 3)
- Consistently stay in touch (System 4)

Keep these systems and practices in place and you will become a follow-up master.

Whenever a sports team is struggling, you'll most likely hear the coach say "we have to get back to the fundamentals." I said at the start of this book that follow-up is one of the fundamentals in the sales process. It's one of the basics. You have to be willing to stay with the fundamentals, the basics, to achieve success. Every action in this system is nothing more than taking care of the fundamentals.

What I've shared with you in this book is not groundbreaking or earthshattering information. It's simply teaching you how to systematically take care of your relationships. In the words of Jim Rohn, it's doing the ordinary things extraordinarily well. That's how you achieve success.

One of my favorite quotes is:

"It's not what you learn, it's not who you know,
it's what you do."

You've taken the time to read this book in its entirety. Now it's time to take action. If you don't start, you'll be no further ahead than you were before you read the book. As I said earlier, to learn new information and put no action behind it has very little value. Decide right now that you're going to change and implement what you've read. If you aren't willing to change now, when will you be? Don't procrastinate. The longer you wait, the more business and relationships you're at risk of losing. Delaying the process will only prolong the pain of not having organization and order in your business and relationships. Don't let another day, week, month or year go by with mediocre practices in place. This is where the pedal meets the metal. I want you to go for it. Get off the sales roller coaster and get away from thin pipelines. Take this book to heart and make changes today!

Goal setting can help you take action, as it gives you focus and purpose. For this reason, I want you to complete a goal-setting exercise so you'll have a clear understanding as to why you need to get this system implemented.

Research has been done that indicates it takes 21 days to form a new habit. As I've said numerous times, using the *Follow Up Sales Strategies System* is nothing more than a habit. Goals are a great support in helping you form your new habits. Set one goal at a time. When that goal has become a habit—hopefully within 30 days—move on to another goal. You don't want to try to develop multiple new habits at one time because that can be overwhelming and when something is overwhelming, we tend not to do it. Be single-minded in your goal-setting approach. Stay committed to the goal at hand.

When setting a goal, it's important to have an understanding as to why you're setting the goal.

Ask yourself the following questions:

- Why is achieving this goal important?
- How will this goal change me once it's achieved?
- What results will I experience from achieving this goal?

These are inquisitive questions and when you can visualize the anticipated accomplishment, it will help you stay motivated and committed to your goal.

You want to be as specific as possible when setting your goals. This will increase your chances of attaining them. For example, you may have a goal to be better at follow-up. While that's a good goal, it's very general. A better goal would be to have the *Follow Up Sales Strategies System* fully implemented by March 31. When you have a timeline, it will move up the accomplishment of that goal on your priority list. When there's no timeline, you're basically saying someday I'll have the *Follow Up Sales Strategies System* implemented. There's no urgency attached to the goal.

It's equally as important to have a plan of action to meet your goal. Follow these three steps and you will have an airtight action plan:

Step #1

Write your goal on paper.

When you write your goal, it moves from a thought in your head to a visual on paper. You can read it on a regular basis, keep it on your desk as a reminder and never lose track of it. If you store the goal in your head, it can easily get lost and forgotten.

Step #2

Write three action steps you can take to accomplish your goal.

When doing this, be careful not to write results. Actions are something you do every day that move you toward your goal.

Using the goal of implementing the *Follow Up Sales Strategies System* by March 31, your three action steps could look like this:

1. Decide on a CRM, purchase it and familiarize yourself with it by February 1.
2. Schedule follow-up time on Fridays for the upcoming week.
3. Stick to my 1, 2, 3 follow-up work system every

workday. I won't end my day until that work has been accomplished.

Step #3

Write 20 reasons why you want to accomplish this goal.

This may seem like a lot, but it's vitally important to understand your desire for setting this goal. This, too, will keep you motivated and committed.

Again using the goal of implementing the *Follow Up Sales Strategies System* by March 31, the reasons why you want to do this could look like this:

1. I want to close more business.
2. I want to be organized.
3. I want to stay in touch with people who are important to me.
4. I want a robust pipeline.
5. I want to exceed my sales goals.
6. I want to be the top salesperson in the company.
7. I want to make more money.
8. I want financial peace of mind.
9. I want to improve my credit score by paying my bills on time.
10. I want to pay off my debt.
11. I want to start saving for my kids' college fund.
12. I want to tithe.
13. I want to start saving for my future.
14. I want to take family vacations.
15. I want more date nights with my spouse.

16. I want to buy a house.
17. I want to travel.
18. I want a beautiful wardrobe.
19. I want a new car.
20. I want to start a new business.

What these reasons reveal is that there's far more to your job or business than just selling a product or service. What you do is about your life. When your business increases, your life changes. This is a very powerful exercise that will help you understand this in a different way. As you write your list, you'll experience feelings of excitement in your core. That's because this list allows you to visualize how you want your life to be and what the possibilities are. All you have to do is get clear about your goal and stay focused on it until it's accomplished.

Something else you can do to keep on track is put a visual on your desk that represents one of your reasons for wanting to achieve the goal. Because life keeps us so busy, it's easy to forget about your goals, but when you have the visual in front of you, it's easy to remember. Keep the visual on your desk, in your car, on the refrigerator, or anywhere else you can easily and frequently be reminded of your goal. Here are some examples of different visuals:

- If one of your reasons is to start traveling and one of your dream trips is going to Italy, you can use a picture of the Leaning Tower of Pisa.
- If one of your reasons is to make more money, you can use a picture of a fancy $ sign.
- If you want to buy a house, you can use a picture of a

beautiful home from a magazine.

- If you want to exceed your sales goals, you can type the number you want to achieve and print it out.

I'm sure you get the idea. When deciding on your visual, make it fun, be creative and make sure it inspires you.

This goal-setting process will work for any goal you want to set, business or personal. It doesn't take very long to complete, so don't start thinking you don't have time. This is your life we're talking about. Of course you have the time.

GOAL-SETTING ACTION PLAN

My 30-day goal is:

Three action steps I can take to achieve my goal:

1.

2.

3.

20 reasons why I want to achieve my goal:

1.

2.

3.

4.

5.

6.

7.

8.

9.

10.

11.

12.

13.

14.

15.

16.

17.

18.

19.

20.

Visual reminders for my reasons:

1.

2.

Some examples of follow-up goals:

- Ask for one referral a day.
- Make one relationship-building contact a day.
- Make one business-building contact a day.
- When following up, call before you email or text.
- Don't make assumptions.
- Implement one of the four follow-up musts.
- Send one handwritten note a day.
- Identify one relationship per week that you've let go and rekindle it.
- Respond to one social media post a day.

For additional reinforcement, I've provided my top 10 follow-up tips. They can also be also be incorporated as goals.

Top 10 Follow-up Tips

1. Decide on one CRM that best fits your needs and use it consistently. A CRM is the heart of an effective follow-up system.
2. When you meet someone and have a connection, reach out the next working day so you can take the relationship to the next level.
3. Say thank you to your customers. They've agreed to do business with you and it's important to show your appreciation.
4. Make a check-in call 30 days after business has been transacted. This call is to see how your customer is doing with your product or service.
5. Stay in touch with your customers a minimum of three

times per year.

6. Make one phone call and/or have one face-to-face meeting per year with your top 20%.
7. Make a "just because" call to your customers for no other reason than to just say hi and see how they're doing. This is always a nice surprise.
8. Say thank you to your referral sources and keep them updated on the referrals they've given you. Take care of those who are promoting you and your business.
9. Remember your customers, prospects, vendors and referral sources on their birthday. Send a card and follow up with a birthday phone call. This gesture will show them you care beyond business.
10. Return phone calls, emails and texts within 24 hours.

I hope this book has motivated and inspired you to look at your business and relationships in a new way. I also hope I've completely changed your perception of follow-up.

I want you to know that I've shared all my practices, tips and secrets with you. I've also shared my successes to help you understand the power of this system. I've held nothing back because I want you to succeed and thrive.

I wish you much success as you go on this new journey!

About the Author

Wanda has been developing systems for corporations for over 25 years. She also has a strong sales background and has worked with sales teams throughout her 25 year corporate career. Teaming these two skills makes her one of the country's leading sales follow up coaches. Wanda teaches workshops to sales teams, offers individual coaching programs and speaks to business organizations and associations.

Wanda had a 25 year banking career where she held the position of Senior Vice President for 15 years. As a banker, she often heard comments from her prospects, customers and referral sources such as ... *"you always call when you say you will", "you always stay in touch" "you never forget my birthday"*. At the time she didn't pay much attention to these comments, but these comments helped her see that, in general, most sales people and business owners struggle in the area of follow up. She saw this is an opportunity and it gave her a mission to build her business knowing how much these skills needed to be taught to others. That's when she decided to share her follow up strategies and proven systems with other business owners, organizations and sales professionals through her company known as *Follow Up Sales Strategies*.

Wanda Allen is a professional speaker who presents on the following topics:

- Your Fortune is in the Follow Up
- 5 Secrets to Closing More Sales with Effective Follow Up
- Exceptional Follow Up & Superior Customer Service

To learn more about Wanda's personalized coaching programs and workshops go to **www.FollowUpSalesStrategies.com**.

Made in the USA
Charleston, SC
02 June 2016